CHIP TALK
PROJECTS IN SPEECH SYNTHESIS

To my loving wife, Kathy

No. 2812
$24.95

CHIP TALK
PROJECTS IN SPEECH SYNTHESIS

DAVE PROCHNOW

TAB BOOKS Inc.
Blue Ridge Summit, PA 17214

TAB BOOKS Inc. offers software for
sale. For information and a catalog,
please contact TAB Software
Department, Blue Ridge Summit,
PA 17294-0850.

FIRST EDITION
FIRST PRINTING

Library of Congress Cataloging in Publication Data

Prochnow, Dave.
Chip talk.

Includes index.
1. Speech synthesis. I. Title.
TK7882.S65P76 1987   621.39'9   86-30097
ISBN 0-8306-1912-7
ISBN 0-8306-2812-6 (pbk.)

Questions regarding the content of this book
should be addressed to:

Reader Inquiry Branch
Editorial Department
TAB BOOKS Inc.
P.O. Box 40
Blue Ridge Summit, PA 17214

Contents

Acknowledgments

IMPORTANT CONTRIBUTIONS WERE MADE BY SEVERAL OUTSTANDING individuals during the preparation of this book. Ms. Mary E. Ottinger of Bishop Graphics, Mr. Bill Stewart of Heath Company, Mr. Gary E. Cox and Mr. Terry Rausin of C-Tron, Mr. Randy Carlstrom of RC Systems, Mr. Larry Pepper of Silicon Systems, Ms. Sherri Capozzoli of Sweet Micro Systems, Mr. Brint Rutherford of TAB BOOKS, Inc., Mr. Tad S. Jones of Votrax, and Mr. George Soluk of VAMP all made generous contributions of their knowledge, equipment, and time.

An even greater appreciation is extended to Ms. Lori Lorenz and her speech students who served as "guinea pigs" for my speech synthesizer projects. Their feedback helped translate the mathematical calculations of speech into the "digestable" schematics found in this book.

Introduction

SPEECH IS PROBABLY THE SINGLE MOST ABUSED ATTRIBUTE OF *Homo sapiens*. We scream at athletic events until our voices are hoarse, we slur our words together during everyday speech and expect listeners to comprehend our utterances, and we continually hurt others through slanderous words. Even with this copious vocal exercise, very few of us understand either the mechanics or the structure of human speech. Our daily aural assaults are a prime illustration of this ignorance.

Even through all of this oral obfuscation many of us strive to extend our own speech. Our reasons for using an artificial voice are varied. A practical reason could be to record a response for a telephone answering machine. A personal reason is possibly to create a synthetic companion. Until recently, the solution to this quest for a disembodied voice has been in magnetic recording media. All you had to do was turn on your portable tape recorder and spend several minutes composing a verbal "letter" to Grandma or making vocal notes about a college lecture. This application was both inexpensive and easy, but there were limitations. For example, once you recorded the phrase "Dear Grandma" on tape, that message remained unchanged until the tape was erased. Therefore, you were unable to make a "boilerplate" message that would satisfy all of your relatives. In this case, each relative would have to be separately addressed and a new message recorded. What you needed was a more versatile method to reproduce your voice.

Recently, an extremely attractive, low-cost method of voice reproduction has been made accessible to the general public. Instead of copying your voice onto a tape, this alternative synthesizes speech from raw sounds. Speech synthesis integrated circuits are able to generate all of the distinct elemental sounds of speech and arrange them into any pattern or word that you desire. By using this method, you could easily alter your message into a personal greeting through only a minor restructuring. Thus, the age of verbal form letters has arrived.

Each of these little silicon "speakers" holds an on-board memory consisting of a minimum of 64 separate and unique speech sounds. By selectively manipulating these 64 building blocks, any word can be synthesized. Furthermore, because of the complexity of these speech chips, an extremely simple synthesizer circuit can be created. That is, each speech integrated circuit is a self-contained vocal mechanism, vocabulary, and processor. All you will need to add to one of these voice simulators is an information controller, a filter, an amplifier, and a power source. Therefore, an inexpensive and fully functional speech synthesizer can be made with a relatively simple construction technique. The only remaining problem is locating these speech chips and figuring out how to build a circuit around them. You are holding the definitive solution to this quandary.

This book contains complete circuit information for building seven powerful speech synthesizers. Each of these projects is based on a different speech synthesis chip and includes a presentation of both stand-alone and computer-based systems. These projects represent working solutions to all of the current approaches to speech synthesis. Therefore, not only will you learn how to construct seven terrific speech synthesizers, but you will also receive an introduction into the technology of speech synthesis.

A brief introduction into human and electronic speech is followed by the seven circuit construction chapters which have been divided into either stand-alone or computer-based synthesizers. All of the projects presented in this book are elementary in their construction. There are also several appendices that will help guide you through any bothersome construction areas. Thus, you will not need either an electronic engineering degree or a toolbox full of exotic tools to complete each circuit. In addition to the typical electronic construction tools, soldering iron, multimeter, pliers, etc., however, you should also purchase a digital logic probe. This small test device is able to identify the current logic status at any test point in your speech synthesizer circuit. You will find that this ability is invaluable when troubleshooting wiring problems in digital circuits.

If you feel that your talents or interests don't fit in the area of electronic circuit construction, this book's final section describes several commercial speech synthesizers. Thus, this book will supply you with two different methods to acquire a speech synthesis capability. All of these products are currently available and each one represents a unique answer to the attainment of intelligible artificial speech. Therefore, the conclusion of this book leaves you with only one question.

/W/ /UH3/ /UH1/ /T/

/AH1/ /UH2/ /ER/

/Y1/ /IU/ /U1/ /U1/

/W/ /A1/ /AY/ /Y/ /T/ /I2/ /NG/

/F/ /O1/ /O2/ /R/?

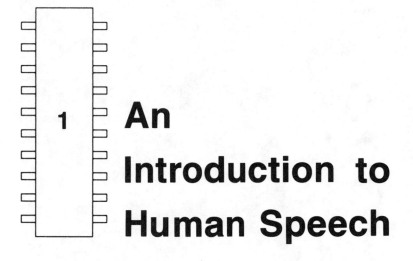

1 An Introduction to Human Speech

HAVE YOU EVER HEARD A FISH TALK? UNLESS YOU ARE THE LOcal town storyteller, your answer to this seemingly ridiculous question would be an incredulous "no." Oddly enough, your skepticism is unjust—in the cases of the freshwater drumfish and the marine grunt. By using various muscular flexures, these two types of fish are able to produce vibrations on their air bladders that result in "voices" and contribute to their odd names. Granted, you might not understand this aquatic language, but the original question didn't query your ability to comprehend this "fishy talk." Interestingly enough, virtually every animal can make vocal sounds. What, you aren't going to question this brash statement? Actually, this unbridled assertion demands a mandatory qualifier.

First, we must define the noun "animal." In this case, we are referring strictly to the vertebrate animals. This would exclude the more numerous invertebrates. Oh sure, the invertebrates have their share of sound-makers. From squeaking earthworms to burping crayfish, the invertebrates are a noisy lot. In fact, the sounds produced by insects such as grasshoppers, crickets, and cicadas are the loudest animal symphony (or cacophony) on earth. Unfortunately, none of these spineless critters can make their clamorous audio performance via their mouth. Instead, each of these noisy orthopterans (the insect order of grasshoppers and crickets) and homopterans (the insect order of cicadas) must rely on either stridulation or tympanic poundings.

The grasshopper (Fig. 1-1) and the cricket use the rubbing together

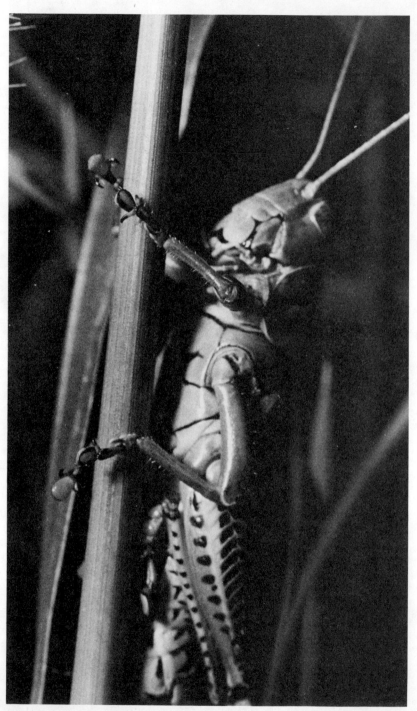

Fig. 1-1. The boisterous grasshopper uses a stridulatory organ for sound production.

of two body parts for the production of their stridulatory sounds. The cicadas, on the other hand, beat a muscular membrane to generate their tympanic sounds. The bottom line of this short lesson in invertebrate communication is that virtually every vertebrate can make *vocal* sounds and the invertebrates, for the most part, can't.

An owl can hoot, a snake can hiss, and a frog can croak, but most of these noises carry very little interpretable meaning in their message. Does this imply that human beings are supreme in their ability to express meaningful vocalizations? Without trying to sound trite, the jury is still out on this decision. The study of higher vertebrate speech patterns is the subject of elaborate research programs that are directed at cetacean communication. Even a casual encounter with a dolphin, porpoise, or whale is usually enough to convince anyone that these marine mammals possess a true spoken language.

Although there is overwhelming evidence to the contrary, many people feel that one "lower" mammal that is capable of meaningful vocalization is the dog (Fig. 1-2). This trusty human companion can bark (protection), yelp (pain), and whine (sorrow). Whether these canine pronounciations are a result of the dog's emotions or an overly zealous application of anthropopathism is a debate that could go unresolved. For the record, however, I KNOW that MY dog is able to communicate with ME. If you wish to continue your pursuit of this subject, a more thorough discussion of vertebrate vocalizations is presented at the end of this chapter.

For the moment, let's ignore the issue of meaningful vocalizations and examine the complexity of vertebrate noises. Let's return to "man's best friend." At most, a dog is able to express half a dozen different emotions through varied sounds. Such a minimal vocabulary is limited in its ability to color the countless subtleties of effective communication. Even the cetaceans and the primates aren't much better off. This total absence of verbose vertebrates means that *Homo sapiens* is the sole "talker" in the animal kingdom. You might ask, what ingredient provides humans with this verbal gift? For once there is a simple answer—the larynx.

THE MAKING OF AN UTTERANCE

Bold statements are usually accompanied by critical objections. The previous question and answer is an ideal example. Many pragmatics would argue that the whole issue of speech cannot be boiled down to one central element like the larynx. They would contend that the vocal cords and their associated resonators and articulators are equal participants in the production of human speech. Others, with a similarly ornery bent for disagreement, would counter this challenge with the point that the larynx is the central attachment site for all of these support components. So, who is right? Without sounding diplomatic, both arguments

Fig. 1-2. Walter, the talking dog has a ''vocabulary'' of six different ''words.'' Unfortunately, he can't apply them in a meaningful fashion.

have valid points. The larynx isn't the sole speech production organ, although its role is vital in the complete speech picture. Likewise, the majority of the organs that are directly responsible for speech are centrally located in the region of the larynx. Regardless of which theory you subscribe to, the larynx is a key figure in human speech. Therefore, our study of the biology of human speech begins with the larynx.

The *larynx* is a cartilaginous box that rests below the base of the tongue and above the trachea. This positioning places the larynx in the direct air flow of everyday breathing. Every breath that travels to the lungs must pass through the larynx.

There are a total of four primary pieces of cartilage that comprise the larynx: the cricoid cartilage, the dual arytenoid cartilages, and the thyroid cartilage. Each of these bits of tissue serves an essential role in the production of human speech.

On the lower back wall of the larynx is the signet ring-shaped cricoid cartilage. This broad-sided piece of cartilage forms the support base of the larynx. On top of the cricoid's elevated back side are the twin arytenoid cartilages. These small triangular cartilages are attached with flexible joints that permit sliding and rotating. Finally, at the top of the larynx is the thyroid cartilage. This v-shaped piece of cartilage articulates at two points with the cricoid. These attachments grant a minor degree of rocking in the physical adjustment of the larynx's shape. One function of the thyroid cartilage is that of protection of the larynx from accidental outside damage. An interesting sidelight of the thyroid is found in its nickname. The thyroid cartilage is also called the Adam's apple. Oddly enough, while the thyroid cartilage is present in both men and women, this popular name is usually applied to its more noticeable projection found predominantly in men.

Stretched across the inner walls of the larynx are the *true vocal cords*. These muscular tissue bands have their attachment points on the arytenoid cartilages and the inside front of the thyroid cartilage. Another set of non-speech related tissue bands are above the true vocal cords and these are sometimes called the *false vocal cords*. Based on the presence of the true vocal cords inside the larynx, it is easy to comprehend the application of the name "voice box" to the larynx.

In order to make speech, the true vocal cords must be suitably positioned in the flow of air through the larynx. This is where the movable arytenoids come into play. Without this ability for vocal cord placement, the vocal cords would permanently obscure the larynx's air passage and vocalizations would be made with every breath that you take. Therefore, the vocal cords partially block the air flow only during *phonation* (speech).

This blockage makes the vocal cords vibrate as the air passes through the larynx. It is this vibration that generates the sound waves which constitute human speech. A leading theory on the actual process espouses air pressure as the leading cause for vocal cord vibration. According to this theory, air pressure increases under the tightly closed vocal cords forcing the cords to break their seal and release a small portion of air. The cords then reseal themselves until the air pressure again forces their separation. This entire sequence is quickly repeated over and over to create a vibration.

Different speech qualities can be produced by altering the shape of the vocal cords prior to their vibration. For example, a tightly stretched vocal cord pair will make a higher pitched sound. Conversely, a set of loose or relaxed vocal cords will produce a lower pitched sound. Speech variations are also possible through the size and shape of the larynx. A smaller larynx will generally have a higher pitch. Women have a smaller larynx which contains shorter vocal cords, and thus have a higher pitched voice. Men, on the other hand, have a larger larynx, which contains longer vocal cords, and normally have a deeper voice. An interesting sidelight to these adult vocal generalizations is found in prepubescent children. In this case, the voices have a virtually identical pitch due to a similar larynx and vocal cord structure. However, after puberty, a young boy's larynx begins to enlarge and increase the length of the vocal cords. Soon his voice will deepen and his adult vocal characteristics will be formed.

Other factors that affect the final sound quality of human speech are found in the resonators and the articulators. The resonators are sound amplifiers that color the final vocal tone. There are three resonators in the human body: throat, nose, and mouth. Granted, the chest, lungs, and diaphragm play a part in resonance. But their role is a minor one in comparison to that of the varied sizes and shapes that are found in human throats, noses, and mouths. It is easy to understand how these resonators contribute to an individual's unique vocalization.

While the resonators color the tones of speech, it is the articulators that serve to separate a clear speaker from a "mush mouth." The palate, tongue, teeth, and lips are the primary speech articulators. The selective placement of these articulators manipulate the air flow for the enunciation of consonants.

In the complete vocal mechanism, the resonators characterize the production of vowels and the articulators form the consonants. The resonators add body to the weak vowel sounds as they enter the throat. The resulting sound is that which we call a vowel. In order to turn that same vocal cord vibration into a consonant, the articulators must take the sound wave and disrupt its flow. The resulting sound is that of a consonant. Repeat this process several thousand times a minute and you will have human speech. But these are only the biological mechanics of speech. What are the actual results of these modified vocal cord vibrations?

PROPER SPEAKING

Basically, the ultimate result of these resonated and articulated vocal cord vibrations is human speech. The emphasis here is on the word "ultimate." There are five additional elements that contribute to good speech. In this case, we will define good speech as understandable utterances. Speech pathologists who were hoping for an in-depth coverage of philology, semasiology, and etymology will have to bite their collective tongue. These studies are beyond the scope of this book.

THE ELEMENTS OF GOOD SPEECH

Breathing. The "cornerstone" of good speech is breathing. As mentioned earlier, breathing is the very basis for speech. Breathing can be broken down into two steps: inhalation and exhalation. Of these two steps, the exhalation is the most critical. It is during the expulsion of a breath that complete mastery of speech is gained. A controlled breath must be maintained for accurate vowel and consonant phonation throughout the duration of the spoken noise, word, or sentence. Inhalations, however, can be "grabbed" during the natural pauses of speech without any regard for their measure (although enough air must be inhaled to provide the necessary energy for phonation).

Try this experiment in breathing. Draw in a breath during a three second period. Now slowly exhale this breath for a total of 15 seconds. This exhalation should be both slow and even in its rate. You can also try different variations on this experiment by speaking repeated vowel or consonant sounds during the 15 second exhalation.

Pitch. The natural pitch of a voice is less important than the voice's inflection. As we learned earlier, the natural pitch of a voice is dictated by the physical shape and size of the larynx. Therefore, pitch is an inherent quality that can come under very little conscious control. Another aspect of pitch, however, is inflection. Inflection in speech can spell the difference between a monotonic dialog and an enthusiastic oratory. In good speech, pitch is used to indicate emotion, as well as signal correct pronunciation.

Repeat the following phrase three times, each time by using a monotone, beginning with a high pitch and alternating each word between a high and a low pitch, and beginning with a low pitch and alternating each word between a low pitch and a high pitch.

"What are you doing here?"

Volume. Superficially, volume is just a matter of being heard. Volume can also indicate your emotional "health" during phonation. As a rule, an angry person has a tendency to express their feelings at a higher volume than does a more relaxed person. It is even possible that certain physical disabilities, such as deafness, can affect vocal volume.

Test the effects of reverse volume applications. For example, the next time you and your paramour are locked in an emotional embrace, scream the phrase, "I love you." Alternatively, in the heat of an argument, utter your angry words at a minimal volume. Who knows, this technique might even end your fight.

Velocity. Good speech is composed of measured phonation bracketed by appropriate pauses. Short pauses indicate a rapid speech pattern and long pauses mark a slower speech rate. There is a fine line of distinction between pauses that are too long and pauses that are too short. Usually, the speaker must alter velocity to match both the subject matter and the audience. For example, a high velocity is characterized as humorous (e.g., certain TV commercials and numerous song lyrics) and a slow velocity is thought of as painful and boring.

Locate a willing test subject. Read two similarly sized, but different paragraphs from this book. First, use an extremely high velocity. Second, read another paragraph at a greatly reduced velocity. When you have finished, ask two questions of your test subject. One, what is your emotional reaction to each reading? Two, what information did you obtain from each paragraph?

Quality. The timbre of the voice is called its quality. Speech timbre is governed by its overtones. These higher tones serve as the unique signature for everyone's voice. Twang, nasal, lisp, and drawl are each different speech qualities. Like many of the other elements of good speech, quality can be altered for a more desirable timbre.

Once again, locate a suitable test subject. Taking turns, each of you should speak the following words. Alter the quality or timbre of each word and have the other person identify the quality that you used.

owe, rye, cow, singing, donate, hoe, lips, drift

SPEECH PARTS

At this point, we know the biology of speech (or, at least we have a firm introduction into this field) and we understand the elements of speech. One final area of speech that will help us in our subsequent electronic speech synthesis studies is phonetics. Basically, *phonetics* is the study of speech sounds. These elemental speech sounds are also known as phonemes. The *d* in "did" and the *s* in "less" are examples of phonemes. An important attribute of phonemes is that they constitute the differences found in the diverse languages of the world. Languages, such as German, Italian, and Spanish, adhere to a rule of simple phonetics. On the other hand, as any first grade student can tell you, the English language is the leading abuser of phonemes.

As with any technical field, phonetics has its own special jargon. In the case of phonetics, this jargon manifests itself as a descriptive symbology. Odd looking, unique characters are used to represent the multitude of sounds that are possible in human language. A valuable fringe benefit of spelling and writing words phonetically is that confusion over the pronunciation of similarly spelled sounds is completely eliminated. For example, the *ou* in "though" and the *ou* in "through." Both of these sounds are spelled the same, but they each bear a different phonetic sound.

In phonetics, there are three types of speech movements: continuants, stops, and glides (this is in relation to the study of human movements or kinesiology). Within these three divisions are the vowels, fricative consonants, nasals, plosive consonants, and diphthongs. Vowels, fricative consonants, and nasals belong to the continuants. Plosive consonants can be plugged into the stops category. Finally, the glides are composed of the diphthongs (see Table 1-1). The following definitions will help in explaining the interrelationships between the speech movements and their phoneme products.

Continuants. The prolonged holding to an initial phoneme is a continuant.

Vowels are open sounds which are amplified with the vocal mechanism's resonators. *a, e, i, o,* and *u* are vowels.

Fricative consonants are consonants articulated through a frictional passage. *ʃ, v, th, s, z, sh,* and *h* are fricative consonants.

Nasals are consonants or vowels exhalated through the nose. *m, n,* and *ng* are nasals.

Stops. The blocking or unblocking of the air flow through the larynx is a stop.

Plosive consonants are formed by completely stopping the articulation of a consonant. *b, d, p,* and *t* are plosive consonants.

Glides. The continuous movement of the vocal mechanism from one phoneme to another is called a glide.

Table 1-1. The Classification of Speech Sounds.

Continuants	Vowels
	Fricative Consonants
	Nasals
Stops	Plosive Consonants
Glides	Diphthongs

Diphthongs form by gliding from the articulatory position of one vowel to the articulatory position of another. *au* and *oi* are diphthongs.

A SLIP OF THE TONGUE

Even after all of this scholarly attention to the physical attributes of speech, vocal errors are bound to occur. In the case of speech, an error is colloquially referred to as a "slip of the tongue." No doubt you are fully qualified, at this time, to dispute the accuracy of this cliche. Nevertheless, faulty phoneme selection, articulation, and arrangement can lead to some humorous phonation moments (or deeply embarrassing ones, depending upon which side of the tongue you are on).

Three of the most visible tongue traps are: tongue twisters, spoonerisms, and Freudian slips. Other verbal faux pas, such as lexical substitution, are more the result of mental error than poor phonation. Granted, a similar argument could be built against the inclusion of Freudian slips. In this case, the Freudian slip is being included due to the large public interest in the theories of Freud.

Say the following phrase ten times, at your fastest rate, "Toyboat." Now, repeat "Rubber baby buggy bumpers," three times. Finally, say "Slick slip knot trick Nick," without spitting all over this page. Your vocal mechanism has just entered the tongue twister zone. A tongue twister is a series of consonants that resist fluid articulation. These tongue contortions are innocent enough and usually inhabit the entertainment domain.

Spoonerisms, however, are verbal gaffes that can, and do, happen at the least desirous opportunity. Take, for example, the stock analyst who reports that, "... the grice of pold," had reached an all-time high. Of course, this bewildered broker meant to say "... the price of gold." A spoonerism is the transposition of the initial phonemes from two or more words. Therefore, instead of asking someone to go "downstairs" you will inadvertently request them to go "stowndairs." An interesting theory on the occurrence of spoonerisms states that each person has a phoneme buffer that holds our future utterances while we are speaking. It is in this phoneme buffer that the transposition is formed and the spoonerism is made.

Concluding our brief sojourn into vocal miscues are the theories of Freud (see Appendix E). In reference to slips of the tongue, these errors are called Freudian slips. Briefly, Freud concluded, after a study of over 90 different cases, that vocal slips developed from the clash of two opposing thought patterns. The first thought pattern is the actual meaning that the speaker desires to convey. Freud called this first thought pattern the *conscious intention.* The second, and much more ominous, thought pattern is a contrary opinion that can reflect the speaker's true feelings. This second thought pattern was labeled as the *disturbing intention* by

Freud. An example of this vocal conflict can be found during the opening address at a symposium, where the keynote speaker greets the audience with, "Thank you for leaving." Of course, the chagrined speaker meant to say, "Thank you for coming."

For the most part, Freud's theories are currently under heavy criticism. Contemporary experimentation is unable to support many of his claims. One of the primary reasons for this discrepancy could stem from the language that Freud studied. His principal tongue was German. Therefore, all of his examples and support references are from German. For example, we, as English readers, find it difficult to appreciate the slip of "temptations" for the word "experiments." In German, however, this error is much more understandable as temptations becomes "Versuchungen" and experiments is "Versuche." Granted, this explanation is thin in its support, but it does offer a plausible accounting for lending credibility to Freud's theories.

TALK TO THE ANIMALS

Earlier in this chapter, we made a good case against non-human

Fig. 1-3. "Psst, did you see that funny looking human?" Some mammals, such as rabbits and giraffes, rarely make the presence of their vocal cords known.

speech. Basically, this vocal exclusivity stems from the presence of specific larynx configurations (e.g. supralaryngeal vocal tract variations) in human beings and the lack of such in other animals. But there is considerable evidence for supporting a claim for the presence of animal languages (see Fig. 1-3). The distinction that must be made here is that none of these animal languages are able to duplicate either the sound or the complexity of human speech.

Conversely, the human language has gone to great lengths to accommodate animal languages. For example, words like whinny, chirp, tweet, and meow are all part of the human vocabulary. These words are used to duplicate animal sounds. Oh sure, if you say chirp, chirp, tweet, chirp to a House Sparrow you won't start any meaningful dialog. The point here is that these representative words serve as mimicry. This same argument applies to certain mimetic birds. These birds are not able to simulate the acoustic or the biological aspect of human speech. They can, however, imitate the sounds of human speech. This interrelationship between acoustics and biology is the foundation of the acoustic theory of speech production.

Fig. 1-4. Several physical differences prevent primates from verbally speaking with us.

All of this discussion boils down to the definitive question, why can't apes speak? Philip Lieberman, Edmund Crelin, and Dennis Klatt (see Appendix E) have proposed four reasons as to why the primates are unable to duplicate human speech (see Fig. 1-4). First, the primate's tongue rests totally inside the oral cavity. In adult humans, the rear third of the tongue forms the anterior wall of the supralaryngeal pharyngeal cavity. Their second point concerns the soft palate and epiglottis. In man, they are widely separated and can't be approximated (or brought together). Conversely, in primates these two structures can be approximated. In the third point, the primate's opening of the larynx into the pharynx is directly behind the oral cavity. In adult humans the opening occurs much further down in the pharynx. Finally, the fourth point addresses the positioning of the vocal cords. In primates, the resting vocal cords are near the fourth cervical vertebra. In adult humans, on the other hand, this resting spot is between the fifth and sixth cervical vertebra and located in a longer neck.

What does all of this mean? Exactly what you already knew; that apes can't talk. Curiously enough, the first three points by Lieberman, et al are also found in infant humans. This statement isn't as shocking as you might at first believe. How many babies that you know can speak in their first few months of life? The answer, like that of the talking apes, is none. The one point, however, that separates the newborn from the primates is the placement of the vocal cords (Lieberman, et al's fourth point). Therefore, you can rest assured that your next son or daughter won't be scampering around the house uttering "oh, oh" when they are 20 years old.

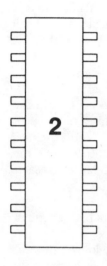

2   An Introduction to Electronic Speech

WHAT IS THIS WORLD COMING TO? YOU PLACE A TELEPHONE CALL to your favorite restaurant for evening reservations and a "voice" on the other end tells you that the restaurant's number has been changed. You go to the grocery store and all of your labeled food is run through a scanner that "tells" you the price of each item. Finally, you're about to take a photograph of your youngster's first pony ride, while the camera "talks" you through the entire procedure. Granted, these encounters themselves are not that bizarre, but the vocalizations that accompany them are otherworldly.

In each of these cases, and hundreds of others just like them, the vocal guidance that you received is *not* being produced by a human voice. Instead, each of these utterances are derived from the digital production of phonemes that are then suitably arranged into distinct words, phrases, and sentences. This digital phoneme production is usually under the direct supervision of a microprocessor unit (MPU). Using an operation that is identical to that of a microcomputer, this MPU-based phoneme generator can access and control the pitch, volume, velocity, and quality of its library of speech sounds. In effect, the resultant sounds from these digitally produced phonemes are very similar to the sounds that are produced through human speech. This is the world of electronic speech synthesis.

In the eyes, or should that be ears, of a speech synthesizer circuit, speech is viewed, or heard, as an analog signal. Conversely, all electronic

MPU-based phoneme production circuits deal strictly in digital signals. Therefore, in the overall scheme of speech synthesis, the desired analog speech pattern must be translated into digital data, suitably arranged and processed by an MPU, converted back into an analog signal, and, finally, "spoken." Luckily, with today's technology, all of these steps are executed under the silicon cover of a single large-scale integrated circuit (LSI). Therefore, the potential speech synthesist is only left with a concern for the construction of a suitable support circuit (and the bulk of this book is devoted to these construction projects).

This simplicity in design hasn't always been the case with speech synthesizers. Back in the late 1930's, Bell Telephone Laboratories performed several extensive experiments in the synthesis of human speech. Their effort was collectively known as the Vocoder. The Vocoder was an enormous circuit that first analyzed a human speech pattern through a series of filters. These electronic filters produced a spectrum of the speech signal which could later be sent to a synthesizer circuit for reconstitution. An important point to remember about the Bell Laboratories' Vocoder, however, is that this circuit required the input of actual human speech for successful operation. This procedure is distinctly different from today's speech synthesizers which artificially create their speech. As an aside, several of the scientists who worked on the Vocoder project tried to send artificially generated signal spectra to the Vocoder's synthesizer. Most of these attempts concluded with modest success, although there was no commercial application of their techniques. These experiments did, however, lay the foundation for the current generation of speech synthesis ICs (integrated circuits).

One last stop in this ancient history of speech synthesis is with Haskins Laboratories. This group took the artificial spectrum input experiments of the Bell Laboratories team and expanded on its potential applications. By using sound spectrograms, Haskins Laboratories was able to produce understandable utterances. An exciting attribute of the sound spectrograms used by Haskins Laboratories was that these spectrograms could be created artificially. Unfortunately, the preparation of these synthetic spectrograms was laborious and the speech quality was minimal. Ultimately, the spectra of the Vocoder gave way to the algorithms of the phoneme.

YES, BUT CAN IT TALK?

In current speech synthesis technology, there are four different methods for producing digital speech: formant synthesis, linear-predictive coding, pulse-code modulation, and adaptive differential pulse-code modulation. Although some sources would treat both pulse-code modulation and adaptive differential pulse-code modulation under the same heading, waveform coding schemes, several important differences make these two speech synthesis methods distinct.

FORMANT SYNTHESIS

Formant synthesis is the most primitive of the speech synthesis techniques. Basically, through formant synthesis, a circuit representation of the entire vocal mechanism is reproduced. By using signals from various frequency generators, the resonators and articulators of the human vocal mechanism are simulated. This final speech product is actually composed of formants. These formants are resonance bands which duplicate the phonetic quality of the prescribed sound. Phoneme synthesis is the most commonly encountered form of formant synthesis.

In the case of phoneme synthesis, these resonance bands are derived from phonemes. ICs that use phoneme synthesis assign a binary code to each of the phonemes contained inside the chip's ROM (read-only memory). During speech production, the user sends the IC a series of binary codes that represents the desired phoneme sequence. The resulting word, phrase, or sentence is composed of these phoneme strings. By and large, speech production with the phoneme synthesis method requires a binary data stream of approximately 70-400 bps (bits per second). An example of a phoneme synthesis IC is the Votrax SC-01.

LINEAR-PREDICTIVE CODING

Linear-predictive coding is a slightly elevated derivative of formant synthesis. Similarly, linear-predictive coding (LPC) duplicates the human vocal mechanism through frequency generators. A major departure from the encoded phonemes of formant synthesis lies in LPC's use of digital filters. Filter coefficients and delays control the filter's multipliers. The predictable nature of these coefficients contributes to this method's name. As a rule there are approximately 10-15 coefficients that must be manipulated. Prior to generation of the phoneme, the filter's coefficients must be suitably excited. These excitation frequencies usually derive from either a white noise or a periodic noise source. Therefore, the complete cycle for an LPC circuit begins with the setting of the proper filter coefficients, followed by the noise source which excites the filter into the production of the phoneme. As it stands, this LPC circuit lacks considerable flexibility. What it needs is greater fluidity.

In order to better duplicate the actions of the human vocal mechanism, an LPC circuit's filter is undergoing constant change. This time-varying filter places increased demands on the design of the overall speech synthesizer. Both memory and speed of transmission are important to these variable LPC filters. For illustration purposes, assuming that the LPC filter needs 4 data bits (or one nibble) assigned to each filter coefficient, another data nibble will represent the phoneme's amplitude, and a final nibble will provide the pitch, there will be 48-68 bits of information for each second of speech. Along these same lines data transmission would have to be 2400-3400 bps. Under more realistic conditions, however, LPC circuits can operate within a transmission range of 100-2400 bps.

There are several ways in which this data transmission rate can be reduced to a more reasonable level. One of the best techniques for this speed reduction is in a minimal encoding system. This technique, however, would also contribute to a degradation in the output speech quality. A second transmission reduction technique involves the addition of an extra parity bit. While the addition of an extra data bit might, at first, appear to be burdening the memory, this parity bit can be used to reduce the effective transmission rate. Actually, this extra bit serves as a warning flag that the speech data is being repeated. Therefore, the filter need only "read" this parity bit to hold its previous utterance. The last transmission retardant involves using the other data bits as special occurrence flags. In other words, the nibbles for amplitude and pitch could be used for marking the presence of non-data intensive pauses. Using this technique, an amplitude of zero (0000) would signal the presence of a pause, while the value for the pitch would indicate the duration of the pause. This final technique would eliminate the need for sending the remaining filter coefficient data. An example of an LPC IC is the Texas Instruments TMS5110A.

PULSE-CODE MODULATION

An actual human voice is digitized, stored, and played back with the method of pulse-code modulation. One quick drawback to the pulse-code modulation (PCM) method is that the digitized data is not stored in a compressed state (ADPCM, on the other hand, is). This lack of data compression takes a heavy toll on the amount of memory that is required for storing several seconds of speech.

During operation, PCM samples pulse codes over an analog waveform's fixed range. This process, which is called quantization, divides the wave's original range into smaller subranges and assigns unique values to each of these newly created subranges. After the values of these subranges have been determined and digitally stored, they are available for analog playback. As the digital signals are recreated into their original analog form, they are transmitted in a series of pulse codes. This process leads to the title of pulse-code modulation.

There are three application limits on the sampling rate used in PCM. The leading theory on these applications limits is the Nyquist interval. Essentially, the Nyquist interval states that the selected rate must be double that of the highest frequency that is to be sampled. For example, if your input signal has a frequency of 3 kHz (kilohertz), then a sampling rate of 6 kHz will adequately cover all frequencies up to 3 kHz. Of course, these theoretical applications are established under optimal conditions. Using the circuits that we will be able to design in this book, a modified Nyquist interval of 4 times (4x) will be much more applicable.

Another application limit centers on the selection of the analog/digital (A/D) converter. This converter takes the sampled rate and changes the analog waveform into digital data. Since A/D converters operate in a climate of fixed gradients there is a possibility for resolution errors. For example, a 4-bit A/D converter is able to resolve a total of 16 steps or gradients ($2^4 = 16$), an 8-bit A/D converter contains 256 steps ($2^8 = 256$), and a 16-bit A/D converter resolves 65536 different steps ($2^{16} = 65536$). As you can see from these three A/D converter examples, the smaller the bit width of the converter, the greater the possibility for a major sampling error. The error that is associated with these A/D converter steps is called the quantizing error. Obviously, the more steps that are present, the less chance there will be for a major speech error. Quantizing error can be calculated with the following formula:

$$Q = VR/2^n \text{ where}$$

Q—the quantizing error
VR—the voltage range of the sampled wave
n—the bit width of the A/D converter

The final application limit deals with the data rate. A PCM speech synthesizer's final data rate can be calculated with the following formula:

$$DR = S * BW$$

DR—data rate
S—sampling rate
BW—A/D converter bit width

Using two of the above parameters, a 6 kHz sampling rate and a 16-bit A/D converter, the final data rate would be a sizzling 96000 bps. This high data rate would not only tax the transmission abilities of many home personal computers, it would also consume great quantities of the computer's memory (roughly 5 seconds of speech would fit into 64K bytes of memory). You can, however, realize a considerable savings in memory, not to mention transmission speed, by using a smaller bit width A/D converter. Using the same sampling rate from the above example and an 8-bit A/D converter results in a reduced data rate of 48000 bps.

As mentioned during the introduction to the PCM method of speech synthesis, the lack of data compression is a serious handicap. In other words, the data is stored exactly as it is received. Steps can be taken to reduce this limitation. First, we need to make an assumption about speech waveforms. As part of our assumption, let's state that speech is composed of varying pitches that display a gradual change. Another part of our pitch assumption is based on the variation in signals between contiguous samples. We shall assume that these signals show a small segment of the overall dynamic range of the recorded vocalization. These assumptions are the basis of a PCM variant called delta modulation (DM). In addition to the above waveform assumptions, DM also uses only a single bit for storing each sample. Under normal operating conditions, a DM circuit samples the A/D converter's input and compares the current signal to the previous signal. If the current signal's amplitude is greater than the previous signal's, the DM circuit stores a bit value of 1. Alternatively, a bit value of 0 is stored if the current amplitude is less than the previous amplitude.

Unfortunately, DM does have some limiting factors that can reduce its widespread replacement of PCM. First of all, the data stream must be read out in exactly the same order and at the same rate at which it was recorded. Two other valuable criteria that can affect the final synthesized speech output are: input data rate and variable input amplitude. If the input data rate is seriously retarded, the quality of speech will drop dramatically. Likewise, a fluctuating amplitude will seriously strain the credibility of the DM algorithm. All three of these factors can lead to a noticeable degradation in the final speech output and jeopardize the intended data rate reduction. An example of a DM speech synthesis IC is the National Semiconductor DT1050 Digitalker system.

ADAPTIVE DIFFERENTIAL PULSE-CODE MODULATION

A vast improvement over PCM in the areas of a lower data rate and a higher degree of voice quality is found by using adaptive differential pulse-code modulation (ADPCM) which follows the sampling techniques established with DM, but with a greater refinement during the sampling stages. An intermediary step between DM and ADPCM uses a value to represent the amplitude difference between each successive sample. This technique is called differential pulse-code modulation (DPCM). Theoretically, the previously mentioned DM circuits could be crudely thought of as 1-bit DPCM circuits. In real applications, however, DPCM circuits use more than 1 bit for their waveform representations. In other words, they are differential quantizers with more than one sample level.

Errors can still mar the performance of DPCM circuits. For example, if the difference between the samples is greater than the predetermined DPCM value, speech distortion will be the result. This type of error, known as the compliance error, can only be corrected by restructuring the DPCM sampling procedure. Another method for improving the output signal is through ADPCM. Under identical speech synthesis conditions, ADPCM will use half the bandwidth that will be used by a PCM system.

Basically, ADPCM varies the sampling quantization (the step size) based on the input signal's rate of change. Additionally, a low data rate is enforced. The result is the compression of a 12-bit PCM sample into a 3 or 4-bit ADPCM signal.

Processing an ADPCM signal is far more complex than any of the other speech synthesis methods previously discussed. Figure 2-1 illustrates the basic steps involved in ADPCM speech synthesis. Initially, the input signal is filtered and digitized through an A/D converter. This PCM digital data is compared against a PCM signal estimate which has been determined from the previous sample. The final differential value is encoded according to the current quantization factor. This final value is the ADPCM data. In a 4-bit ADPCM system, this final encoding will result in a 4-bit ADPCM data code. The major difference between this procedure and the one used with DPCM circuits is ADPCM's ability to adjust the quantization based on the current output.

Decoding an ADPCM encoded signal converts the output data back into a differential value by using the same quantization found in the encoding process. Each of these differential values are stored until the original waveform has been restored. A unique feedback loop prevents a system overload due to encoder malfunction. One area that is occasionally overlooked in a PCM-oriented system is a quantization error known as the signal-to-noise ratio (SNR). The SNR can be further exaggerated

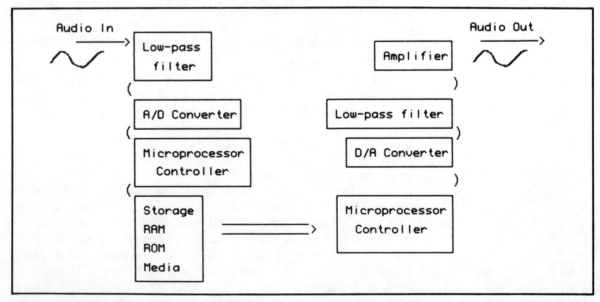

Fig. 2-1. An ADPCM system is able to faithfully duplicate human speech through a series of analog-digital-analog conversion steps.

by the ADPCM encoding and decoding. A signal and PCM quantization error independent SNR can be calculated by:

$$SNR = PCMSNR \div (1 + PCMSNR \div ADPCMSNR)$$

SNR—system signal-to-noise ratio
PCMSNR—PCM input SNR
ADPCMSNR—ADPCM SNR

By using this formula, the best SNR is obtained by matching the PCM SNR to the ADPCM SNR.

While the choice between A/D converter bit width was vital in reducing the data rate in PCM circuits, the choice between 3-bit and 4-bit ADPCM circuits is negligible. Granted, the greater the number of sampled bits, the larger the reduction in SNR. In actual practice, however, the increased SNR results in only a slight alteration in the output speech quality. An example of an ADPCM IC is the Oki Semiconductor MSM5218RS.

ELECTRONIC VOCABULARY

Understanding the mechanism of speech synthesis is only half the battle. In practical terms, true speech output is the war. An IC with the ability to utter perfect phonemes is a marvel of technology, but organizing these phonemes into intelligible words, phrases, and sentences is the ultimate goal. This organization amounts to nothing more than translating a desired word into a selectable phoneme code string. For example, by using the phonemes of the Votrax SC-01, the word "Tab" becomes:

TAE1EH3B

This unusual looking string of alphabetic and numeric characters is composed of four different SC-01 phonemes— T / AE1 / EH3 / B. Each of these phonemes is assigned a specific binary code. In binary code, "Tab" looks like this:

101010101111000000001110

Again, breaking this code into its phoneme equivalents, equals— 101010 / 101111 / 000000 / 001110 . Other representations that are designed to aid humans in dealing with binary numbers include:

Hexadecimal- 2A / 2F / 00 / 0E

Decimal- 42 / 47 / 0 / 14

Now our only problem is in sending these codes, in whatever form, to the speech synthesizer. There are four different techniques for controlling phoneme string production: analog switches, RAM, ROM, and EPROM.

Analog Switches. By far, the simplest technique for sending a phoneme code sequence to a speech synthesis IC is by using analog switches, like those in Figure 2-2. There is no need for complex circuitry or the external processing support of a microcomputer. Each phoneme's binary code is individually set with SPST (single-pole, single-throw) switches. This hardware setting is then strobed through the input data port of the speech synthesis IC. The result is the utterance of the coded phoneme. Section I deals exclusively with speech synthesizers based on analog switch phoneme selection.

RAM. Random access memory (RAM) phoneme coding is the most flexible, as well as the most demanding of these four techniques. Under RAM control, phoneme strings are stored in this volatile memory region. This storage can occur either through direct keyboard entry, which is ridiculous for greater than one dozen phonemes, or through software.

Fig. 2-2. The top row of analog switches are used for coding a specific data bit address.

Fig. 2-3. A typical EPROM with the protective cover removed from its erasure window.

Manipulating the phoneme strings via software demonstrates the superior flexibility of the RAM technique. Of course, this form of phoneme control does require a fluency in programming. The greatest drawback, however, is that once the computer is turned off, all of the phoneme strings are lost. Granted, you will probably save your phoneme-producing software on a floppy disk, but the point is that RAM phoneme coding is transitory. Section II of this book contains several speech synthesizers that make use of this phoneme coding technique.

ROM. The read-only memory (ROM) technique provides the user with a valuable convenience. Within a factory programmed IC are numerous words and phrases that are ready for use. Each of these preformed phoneme strings is assigned to a specific address inside the IC ROM. Therefore, all the user has to do is select the desired word and send its address to the speech synthesis IC. There is no need to translate the word into phonemes and input the final binary data into a speech chip. All of the phoneme coding is "invisible" to the user. ROM phoneme coding lets the user concentrate on semantics instead of phonetics.

Unfortunately, ROM coding does have a catch. Each of the words

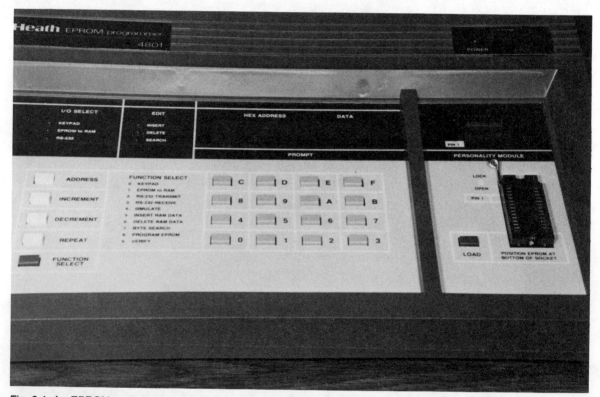

Fig. 2-4. An EPROM programmer, such as this Heathkit model, is ideal for coding your own speech vocabulary into a speech synthesizer circuit.

Fig. 2-5. A powerful UV light inside an EPROM eraser is used for "resetting" an EPROM to a logic of 1. This Heathkit model will hold several EPROMs for simultaneous erasing.

and phrases that are contained within ROM are determined by the manufacturer. If you need a word that is not "burned" into ROM, then you are out of luck. EPROM coding offers a technique for circumventing this limitation.

EPROM. By using some specific equipment, any user can custom program a speech synthesis ROM chip. This technique is known as EPROM (erasable programmable read-only memory) coding. An EPROM is a special ROM chip (see Fig. 2-3) that can be programmed and erased and reprogrammed, over and over again (usually there is a limit of 12 sequences), by the user. This programming is accomplished through bursts of voltage ranging from 12.5 VDC (volts dc) to 24 Vdc (see Fig. 2-4). Each voltage surge causes the EPROM's address logic to change from its erased state of 1 to the programmed logic condition of 0. An EPROM is erased by exposure to concentrated UV (ultraviolet) light (see Fig. 2-5). This erasure changes *all* logic addresses to a state of 1. Therefore, through selective programming, an entire speech vocabulary, one that is unique to your specific application, can be placed in a single EPROM. Figure 2-6 is an example of one of the more common EPROMs.

Without a doubt, EPROM phoneme coding is the superior technique. Its only limitation is the relative scarcity of EPROM programmers with full knowledge of EPROM programming.

WHICH SPEECH SYNTHESIS SYSTEM IS BEST?

Now that you are familiar with the methodology used in speech synthesis, your next question should be: based on the four methods for synthesizing speech, which system is the best? Are you ready for this answer? It all depends on your needs and the desired application. Now this response isn't intended as some clever, middle-of-the-road quip. Under real conditions, both your financial and vocal resolution needs will actually

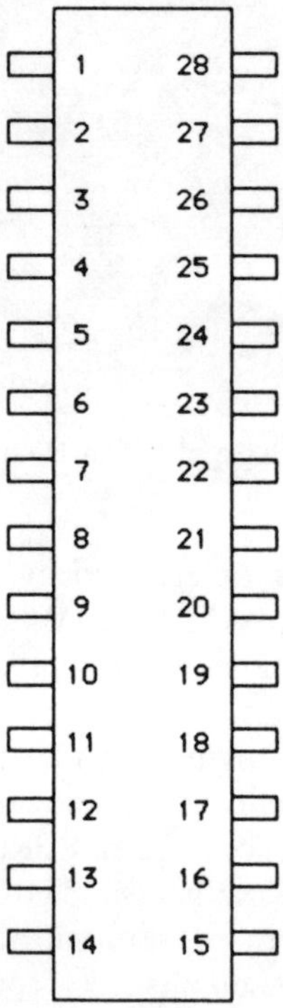

Pin Assignments			
Pin Number	Function	Pin Number	Function
1	V_{PP}	15	03
2	A12	16	04
3	A7	17	05
4	A6	18	06
5	A5	19	07
6	A4	20	$\overline{CE}$
7	A3	21	A10
8	A2	22	$\overline{OE}$
9	A1	23	A11
10	A0	24	A9
11	00	25	A8
12	01	26	A13
13	02	27	$\overline{PGM}$
14	Gnd	28	V_{CC}

Fig. 2-6. Pin assignments for a 27128 EPROM.

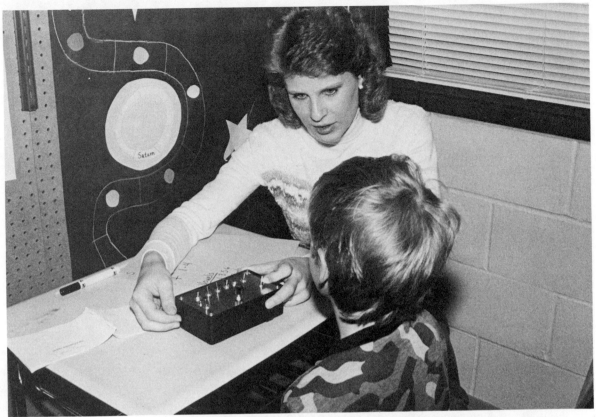

Fig. 2-7. Speech language pathologist, Lori Lorenz, uses a speech synthesizer circuit in long vowel instruction.

dictate your selected speech synthesis method (see Fig. 2-7).

For example, if low cost is your main interest in speech synthesis, then an IC that uses formant synthesis will be your best bet. On the other hand, if you are after the highest degree of speech intelligibility, then the ADPCM route is for you. Between these two extremes lie the other speech synthesis methods. Therefore, your principal decision will be in evaluating your specific needs and matching a speech synthesis method to them. Yes, there are other factors that will color your selection. These problems include whether it is a stand-alone system, a computer-based system, and/or a commercially available system. In consideration for these decision hurdles, the next three sections of this book cover speech synthesizers that provide working solutions to these problems.

Section I

Stand-Alone Speech Synthesizers

IN MANY SPEECH SYNTHESIS APPLICATIONS, THE EMPLOYMENT OF a controlling microcomputer is impractical. Saddling a compact synthesizer circuit with the burdensome bulk of a dedicated microcomputer, even one of the compact portable computers, destroys the spontaneity and flexibility of such a speech design. For example, when operating in a field environment, the presence of power outlets, a controlled atmosphere, and a sizable work area are all nonexistent commodities. In these situations, a speech synthesizer that can function independently of a computer is needed.

A stand-alone speech synthesizer has a few deficiencies when compared to the computer-based circuits. But exactly what is a stand-alone speech synthesizer and how does it differ from the computer-dependent variety?

Basically, a stand-alone speech synthesizer operates independently of an external microprocessor's control. Granted, stand-alone units can be designed with their own on-board microprocessor, but this defeats one of the primary attractions of the stand-alone unit—low cost. The lack of any microprocessor does impose a certain limitation on the stand-alone design. This limitation translates into a fixed operation speed with no provision for successful concatenation. The types of *concatenation*, or element stringing, are structured for the various speech synthesis methods. In other words, with the General Instrument SPO256-AL2 project (see Chapter 3), allophones are the elements that would resist successful stringing. Please don't infer from this discussion that the GI IC is incapable of allophone concatenation. This couldn't be further from the truth. The point is that, without microprocessor control, stand-alone circuits resist concatenation.

The major barrier to stand-alone concatenation is found in the data input interface. Standard, analog SPST (single-pole, single-throw) switches are used for sending the speech data to the IC (see Fig. I-1). Therefore, the flipping of these switches dictates the output from the speech synthesizer. Of course, if you are an extremely fast switch flipper, you might be able to overcome the stand-alone speech synthesizer's resistance to concatenation.

There are two other areas where the stand-alone speech synthesizer has advantages over its computer-based relative. First, the stand-alone version operates from battery power. An exception to this rule is the National Semiconductor DT1050 project (see Chapter 4). By using batteries as a power source, the stand-alone circuit is able to remain light weight and contain a low parts count. This last factor also means that building one of these circuits will cost less than a similarly equipped computer-based version.

Fig. I-1. A bank of SPST switches are used for programming stand-alone speech synthesizers.

The second advantage of the stand-alone unit is in the actual production of the speech output. As a rule, the audio output from a speech synthesis IC must be amplified for use. Adding a small audio amplifier IC (e.g., LM386) to the stand-alone circuit contributes excellent audio performance with only a modest investment in support components. The result is a signal that is capable of driving a small 8-ohm speaker. Therefore, coupling this audio amplifier and speaker arrangement to the stand-alone circuit makes a functional, light-weight, low-cost speech synthesizer.

In this section, you will be given the complete plans for constructing two vastly different stand-alone speech synthesizers. The first project, based on the General Instrument SPO256-AL2, is called The Allophone Maker (Chapter 3). This simple project should be constructed by every reader prior to attempting any of the other speech synthesizer projects contained in this book. Why, you ask? Simply because The Allophone Maker demonstrates all of the construction techniques that will be used in the later projects (see Fig. I-2). It is far easier to learn speech syn-

Fig. I-2. The Allophone Maker circuit ready for final assembly.

thesizer design practices on this simple circuit than it is to comprehend similar techniques when building a complex ADPCM circuit.

The final circuit in this section is The Phrase Maker. This project is centered around the National Semiconductor DT1050. The Phrase Maker is a far more sophisticated project than The Allophone Maker. A special ROM support IC provides The Phrase Maker with a vocabulary of "real" words. This output is completely different from the elemental allophones uttered by The Allophone Maker. Both of these designs will give speech synthesis enthusiasts who lack access to a microcomputer something to /TT2/ /AO/ /AO/ /KK2/ about.

3 General Instrument SPO256-AL2

IF WE REDUCE SPEECH TO ITS BASAL ELEMENT, WE ARE LEFT WITH the phoneme. As we discussed in Chapter 1, the phoneme can effect different pronunciations which are controlled by the phoneme's position within the spoken word. In other words, the aspirated phoneme p in the word "part" sounds different than the nonaspirated phoneme p in the word "spice." Another element of speech that describes these phonemic differences is the allophone.

In a basic sense, the allophone is a variant of two or more similar phonemes. As was demonstrated in the above example, this variation is usually dictated by the position of the phoneme within the spoken word. Therefore, successful allophonic speech synthesis is positional dependent. In "real" synthesis applications, selective allophone placement combined with proper pausing will help in satisfying this positional criterion.

One of the best methods for electronically producing allophones is through formant synthesis (see Chapter 2 for an explanation of formant synthesis). In this method, each of the allophones are encoded and stored in an internal ROM at a specific address. Later, during speech synthesis, a user input allophone address produces the desired part of speech. The main advantage for using this method in allophone synthesis is that an extremely low data bit rate, approximately 60-100 bps, is required for speech production. In fact, a bonus from this low data bit rate is a simplified circuit that is ideally suited to stand-alone operation.

THE SPO256-AL2

The General Instrument SPO256-AL2 IC is an N-Channel MOS (metal oxide semiconductor) LSI (large scale integration) package that uses allophonic formant speech synthesis (see Fig. 3-1). A flat frequency output response of 0-5 kHz, dynamic range of 42 dB, and a SNR of 35 dB are possible. This is a digital output that must be run through a low-pass filter prior to external amplification.

An internal 16K byte ROM contains the allophone set that is used by the SPO256-AL2. Each allophone is assigned to a specific data address that is accessed by a six-bit data input. This six-bit address is capable of manipulating 59 allophones and five pauses.

There are two general modes of operation with the SPO256-AL2.

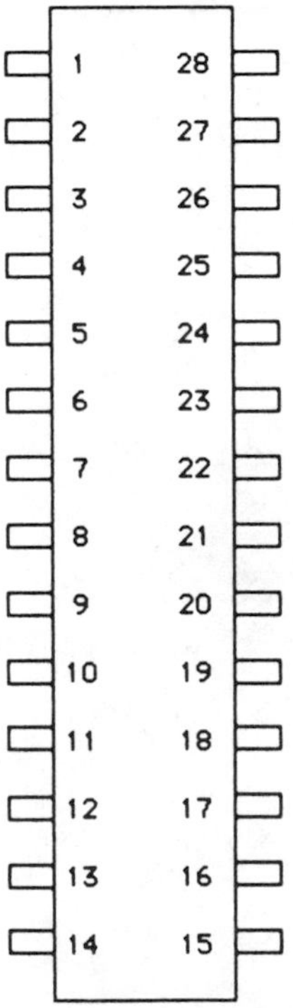

Pin Assignments			
Pin Number	Function	Pin Number	Function
1	V_{SS}	15	A4
2	Reset	16	A3
3	ROM Disable	17	A2
4	C1	18	A1
5	C2	19	SE
6	C3	20	$\overline{ALD}$
7	V_{DD}	21	SER IN
8	SBY	22	TEST
9	$\overline{LRQ}$	23	V_{D1}
10	A8	24	Audio Out
11	A7	25	$\overline{SBY\ RESET}$
12	SER OUT	26	ROM CLK
13	A6	27	OSC 1
14	A5	28	OSC 2

Fig. 3-1. Pin assignments for SPO256-AL2.

Each mode is determined by the status of the Strobe Enable pin (SE, pin 19). When SE has a logic of 0 (SE = 0), an address is loaded for each data bit that makes a transition from low to high. Conversely, when SE has a logic of 1 (SE = 1), an address is loaded from a low pulse on the Address Load pin (ALD; pin 20). This last mode is the address loading technique that is used in this project.

CONSTRUCTION OF THE ALLOPHONE MAKER

Only two ICs are needed in the construction of The Allophone Maker (see Fig. 3-2 and Table 3-1). In addition to the central SPO256-AL2 IC, a support audio amplifier IC (LM386) is used to drive an 8-ohm speaker. The bulk of the parts in this project are current limiting resistors and the components for the low-pass filter.

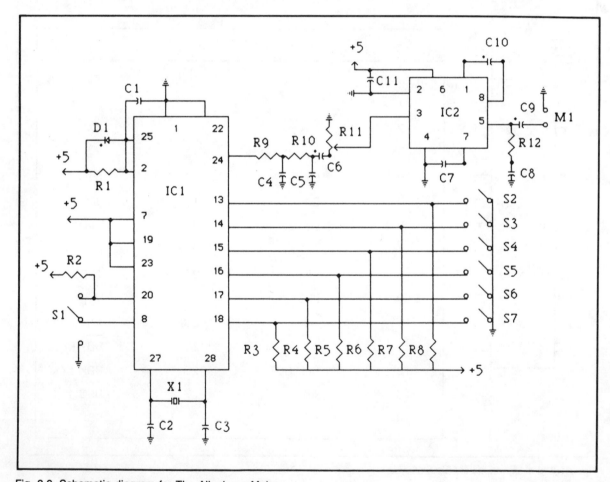

Fig. 3-2. Schematic diagram for The Allophone Maker.

Table 3-1. Parts list for The Allophone Maker.

```
C1, C7, C8, C11 - .1 mf capacitor
C2, C3 - 47 pf capacitor
C4, C5 - .022 mf capacitor
C6, C10 - 10 mf electrolytic capacitor
C9 - 100 mf electrolytic capacitor
D1 - 1N914 Diode
IC1 - SPO256-AL2 Voice Synthesizer IC
IC2 - LM386 Low Voltage Audio Power Amplifier IC
M1 - 8-ohm speaker
R1, R3, R4, R5, R6, R7, R8 - 100K resistor
R2 - 10K resistor
R9, R10 - 33K resistor
R11 - 10K potentiometer
R12 - 10-ohm resistor
S1 - SPDT momentary switch
S2, S3, S4, S5, S6, S7 - SPST switch
X1 - 3.579545 MHz TV colorburst crystal
```

This circuit will easily fit on a 3.5 × 3″ universal PC board with IC spacing (e.g., Radio Shack #276-168). Additionally, a PC board with two bus strips, one for +5 V and another for ground, will reduce construction frustrations. You should also, at this time, determine the nature of your power source. A 6 V, 4 "AA" battery holder is an adequate supply for The Allophone Maker.

Begin your construction by soldering two IC sockets, one 28-pin and one 8-pin (that is, if you are using the 386 audio amp IC), to your selected PC board. On a small PC board, this placement is critical. Therefore, be sure to thoroughly examine your desired socket positions before making the initial solder joints.

After the IC sockets have been installed, add the support components. In order to avoid any confusion, start with the addition of the audio amp components. A successfully completed amplifier section will need the addition of three wires. These wires are: the twin speaker connectors (from pin 5 and ground with a 386 IC) and the output from the 10K potentiometer (pin 3). Ample length should be given to each of these wires with reference to your final assembly container. A length of 6-8″ is about right. One convenient technique for establishing future connection sites, such as with the speaker wiring, is to draw these wires from an isolated section of the PC board. This type of placement will pay dividends when it is time for the final assembly.

Next, all of the support components for the SPO256-AL2 are soldered into place. This includes the low-pass filter from pin 24, the oscillator between pins 27 and 28, and the reset power lead from pins 2 and 25. Also the power and ground connections for pins 7, 23, 19, 1, and 22 can be made at this time. Three more wires will have to be cut and soldered at pins 8 and 20 and ground. This triple wiring is for the SPDT (single-pole, double-throw) switch that loads the data bit address into the SPO256-AL2 for speaking.

This final piece of circuit board wiring can be the most tedious. Six current resistors are attached to pins 13-18 of the SPO256-AL2. These same six pins also independently connect to one pole of six different SPST switches. Finally, the other pole of each SPST switch is tied to ground. It is the setting of these switches that determines the final data bit address.

During the final assembly, all of the wiring connections are made, the necessary holes are drilled in the selected container, and each of the subassemblies (PC board, battery pack, and speaker) are fixed inside the container. You shouldn't dismiss the importance of careful attention in these final assembly steps. Several finishing touches that are appropriate for this type of circuit are a power switch with a matching LED (light emitting diode) indicator lamp, an indexed knob on the amplifier's volume pot, and dry transfer lettering which labels all of switches on The Allophone Maker.

OPERATION OF THE ALLOPHONE MAKER

If you have prepared this project exactly as described above, The Allophone Maker will utter an allophone as soon as the power is turned on if you have the data bit SPST switches set for an allophone's address (see Table 3-2). Try several different switch settings, until you can hear an allophone from the speaker. Failure to hear any allophones can be due to three causes: insufficient volume (solution; turn up the volume), wrong SPST switch settings (solution; try various data settings and switch combinations), and failure to pulse ALD (solution; toggle the SPDT switch to the speak position).

By using the following convention, you will be able to understand the operation of The Allophone Maker better. Label your six SPST switches as 1, 2, 3, 4, 5, and 6 in a linear, left to right fashion. You now have six data bit address switches, each one with its own unique label. If you have soldered your switches in a standard manner (i.e., a switch in the up position is considered "on"), then the representation

1-2-5

indicates that switch numbers 1, 2, and 5 are in the up and "on" posi-

Table 3-2. The Allophones and Their Decimal Addresses of the SPO256-AL2 IC.

Decimal Address	Allophone	Example
0	PA1	Pause
1	PA2	Pause
2	PA3	Pause
3	PA4	Pause
4	PA5	Pause
5	OY	Toy
6	AY	By
7	EH	End
8	KK3	Comb
9	PP	Park
10	JH	Dodge
11	NN1	Bin
12	IH	Bit
13	TT2	To
14	RR1	Rural
15	AX	Succeed
16	MM	Milk
17	TT1	Part
18	DH1	They
19	IY	Be
20	EY	Rage
21	DD1	Would
22	UW1	To
23	AO	Bought
24	AA	Lot
25	YY2	Yes
26	AE	Bat
27	HH1	He
28	BB1	Business
29	TH	Thin
30	UH	Hook
31	UW2	Rude
32	AW	Out
33	DD2	Dew
34	GG3	Pig
35	VV	Vest
36	GG1	Gun
37	SH	Ship
38	ZH	Azure

Decimal Address	Allophone	Example
39	RR2	Drain
40	FF	Fun
41	KK2	Sky
42	KK1	Can
43	ZZ	Zebra
44	NG	Anchor
45	LL	Lose
46	WW	Won
47	XR	Fair
48	WH	While
49	YY1	Yes
50	CH	Charge
51	ER1	Her
52	ER2	Fir
53	OW	Row
54	DH2	Them
55	SS	Best
56	NN2	No
57	HH2	Hoe
58	OR	Gore
59	AR	Alarm
60	YR	Ear
61	GG2	Give
62	EL	Rattle
63	BB2	Buy

tion. Furthermore, this means that the SPO256-AL2 has a logic of 1 on pins 13, 14, and 17. In a binary pattern, this would be:

110010

or, a decimal 50. By applying this switch-to-binary-to-decimal conversion, all of the allophone addresses of the SPO256-AL2 can be easily accessed. Just remember that pin 18 on the SPO256-AL2 is the least significant bit (LSB) and that pin 13 is the MSB (most significant bit), which correspond to switch numbers 1 and 6, respectively.

APPLICATIONS FOR THE ALLOPHONE MAKER

The most dramatic use for The Allophone Maker is in the field of speech pathology. By using this inexpensive and portable unit, the speech pathologist can focus a student's attention on a specific group of trouble-some allophones. A sample of 59 different allophones can be had through the variable switch settings. In the classroom or clinic environment, each of these allophones are spoken at the press of the SPDT switch. Additionally, the final speech sound of each allophone is held, even after the SPDT is released. Therefore, the beginning and concluding elements of each allophone can be analyzed by the student. This partitioning is extremely beneficial to youngsters who lack the finer degrees of sophistication in speech formation.

The amplified sound of The Allophone Maker is ideal for individual learning. Most classroom situations, however, involve several students wishing simultaneous instruction. A solution to this potential dilemma is to incorporate a headphone jack into the design of The Allophone Maker. Through this addition, several sets of simultaneous allophonic instruction can take place in the same classroom.

ONE MORE STEP

There are two circuit alterations that can be incorporated into The Allophone Maker. The first is the addition of two more SPST data bit switches. These dual switches would mimic the installation of the other six (i.e., each has a 100K power resistor on one post and ground on the other), but they would be connected to SPO256-AL2 pins 10 and 11. The addition of these two switches would give you access to 256 speech entry points.

The other circuit alteration involves the addition of an external speech dictionary. This dictionary, which is contained on an EPROM, would be accessed through the six data bit switches. One of the benefits of this external speech EPROM is that you could write your own custom vocabulary. Then each data switch setting would select a preprogrammed allophone string that is stored in the EPROM. In order to have a large base of possible address points within the EPROM, the two extra data bit switches described above, should be added. Programming this EPROM will have to be executed in two separate steps. Step 1 is a special control decoder program that must handle the ASR (automatic send/receive) register, the address decoding, and several other register requirements. The second step is the actual allophonic programming. Once all of these instructions have been programmed, the EPROM can be directly interfaced to the SPO256-AL2. The key word here is to /EH/ /KK1/ /SS/ /PP/ /IH/ /ER2/ /IH/ /MM/ /IH/ /EH/ /NN1/ /TT2/ /PA5/.

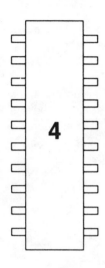

National Semiconductor DT1050 Digitalker

A LONG STANDING COMPLAINT AGAINST SPEECH SYNTHESIS CIR-
cuits has been the mechanical sound of their speech. This factor
is primarily dependent on the method of speech synthesis used by the
circuit. The frequency encoded methods, like that found in the
SPO256-AL2, are the leading "spokeschips" for this highly synthetic
voice. Basically, the selective manipulation of the frequency filters found
on these chips is able to provide an intelligible speech, but it is one that
is devoid of any warmth or human vocal quality.

In the speech synthesis arena, Chapter 2 mentioned PCM and
ADPCM as the most human-like. Both of these methods are able to match
various nuances in human speech by using waveform digitization. By following prescribed sampling rates, the human voice input is analyzed,
stored, and synthesized through a series of A/D, D/A, and low pass filter stages. Building on this basic PCM recording method, data compression is able to increase the output's intelligibility.

Delta Modulation is a common PCM compression method. By storing only the changes in the sampled waveform amplitudes, DM produces
a reduced data bit rate. This reduced data rate in turn means that less
memory is required for word storage.

The National Semiconductor DT1050 Digitalker IC uses a proprie-
tary PCM data compression formula that was developed by Forest Mozer
at the University of California-Berkeley. Mozer's algorithm builds on the

sampling techniques used in DM. Additionally, the DT1050 speech processor chip, MM54104, contributes phase-angle adjustment and half-period zeroing compression to the basic data compression algorithm.

Phase-angle adjustment produces mirror images of a waveform based on half of the waveform's data. The principle behind phase-angle adjustment concerns the phase angle of the sine wave portions of a given waveform. Essentially, the intelligibility of speech is independent of this phase angle. Therefore, an adjustment of these sampled waveform values would use only half of the data for reconstructing this symmetrical image.

Half-period zeroing, on the other hand, stores all low amplitude wave sections as silence. In the case of pitch changes, this technique leaves only the central portion of each pitch change intact. Therefore, the initial pitch rise and concluding pitch fall are both eliminated from the sample. Once again, this saves valuable memory space and reduces the overall data bit rate.

THE DIGITALKER

The National Semiconductor DT1050 Digitalker is a three chip (one speech processor IC and two ROM vocabulary ICs) speech synthesis system. The main speech processor chip, MM54104, is an NMOS LSI device (see Fig. 4-1). A 14-pin address bus and 8-pin data bus are used for communication between the MM54104 and the two ROMs, MM52164SSR1 and MM52164SSR2 (see Fig. 4-2). All of the compressed speech data is stored on these ROM chips. Each ROM chip is a 64K bit NMOS package that can be serially connected for a maximum of 128K bits of PCM speech data. The ROM chips also require less voltage than the 7-11 V range of the MM54104. Both of the ROMs rate a 4.75-5.25 V on pin 24.

Only a minimal number of external connections are necessary to operate the DT1050 chip set. An external filter and amplifier section are attached to pin 39 of the MM54104 for speech output. Likewise, the chip's reference frequency is controlled by an external oscillator connected between pins 1 and 2. The final external connection is with the analog data bit address switches.

The MM54104 is activated by a logic of 0 on the Chip Select (CS; pin 3) pin. The DT1050 is now ready for speech production. After the data bit switches have been set, the Write Strobe (WR; pin 4) is pulsed from a low logic to a high logic and latches this address. The current logic of the Command Select (CMS; pin 7) determines the subsequent action. A logic of 0 resets the system interrupt and initiates the speech sequence. A logic of 1 on CMS causes a reset interrupt. The ROM chips return the word corresponding to the selected address and send the expanded data to pin 39 (Speech Out) for output.

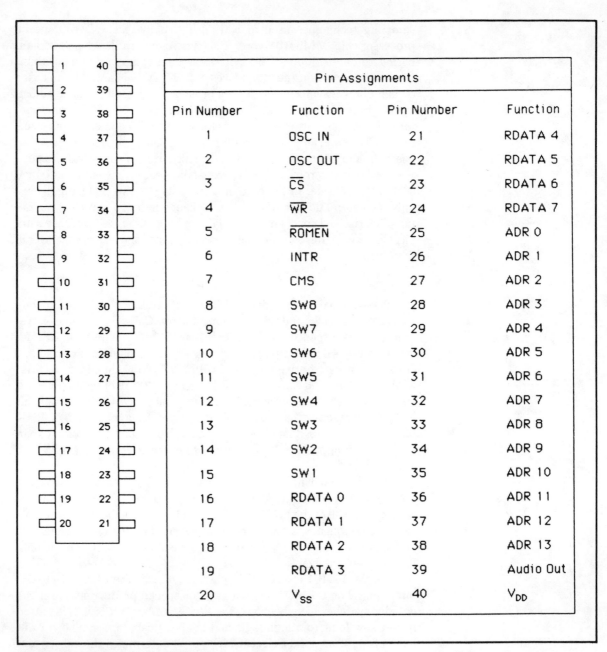

Fig. 4-1. Pin assignments for MM54104.

CONSTRUCTION OF THE PHRASE MAKER

A total of five ICs are used in the construction of The Phrase Maker (see Fig. 4-3 and Table 4-1). While the two ICs that constitute the filter/amplifier section are small 8-pin DIPs, the three chip DT1050 set is a monstrous PC board space-waster. The two ROM chips are each 24-pin packages and the MM54104 speech processor chip is a 40-pin device. Therefore, you will need a PC board that is at least 4.5 × 7" (e.g., Radio Shack #276-190) to hold the five IC sockets, support components, and necessary wiring.

Many potential wiring headaches can be avoided if you use a PC board that has 2 bus strips. With this type of PC board, one of the buses can be used for the +5 V and the other can be used for ground. An additional complication is found in the voltage requirements for the MM54104, however. This IC has a voltage tolerance of 7-11 V. Therefore, all logic 1 pins (e.g., the data bit address switches in the "on" position) and the chip's main power supply pin (pin 40) need to receive this unique voltage. One solution would be to assign one of the bus strips to this 7-11 V and the other bus strip to ground. Then, the few connections that re-

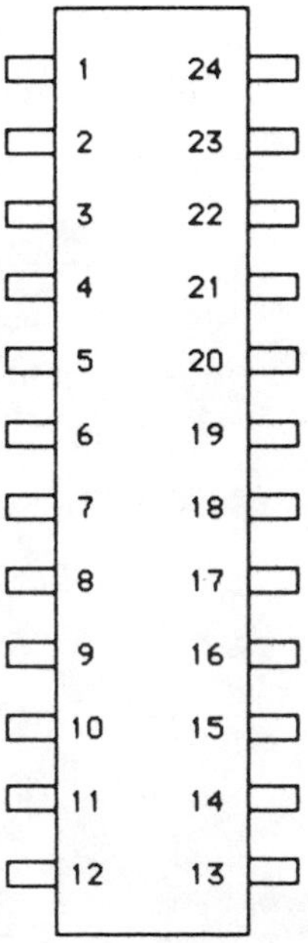

Pin Assignments			
Pin Number	Function	Pin Number	Function
1	A7	13	04
2	A6	14	05
3	A5	15	06
4	A4	16	07
5	A3	17	08
6	A2	18	A11
7	A1	19	A10
8	A0	20	CS1 (A13)
9	01	21	A12
10	02	22	A9
11	03	23	A8
12	Gnd	24	V_{CC}

Fig. 4-2. Pin assignments for MM52164SSR1/2.

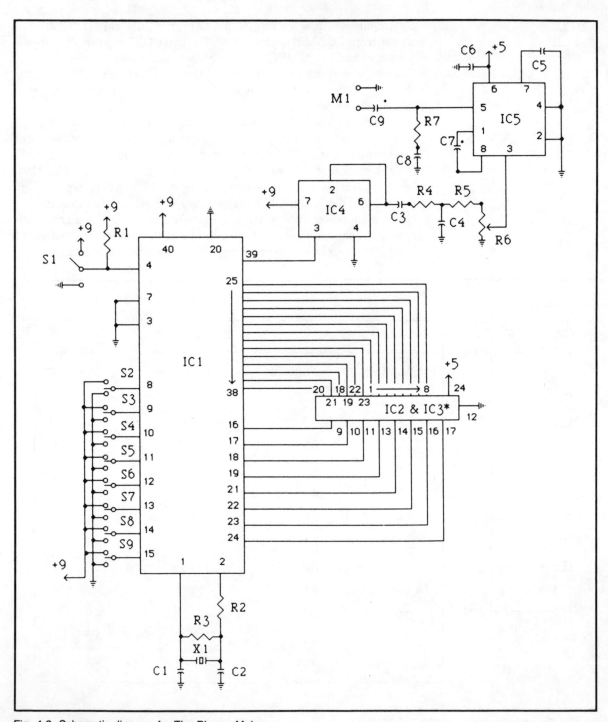

Fig. 4-3. Schematic diagram for The Phrase Maker.

Table 4-1. Parts List for The Phrase Maker.

```
C1 - 47 pf capacitor
C2 - 100 pf capacitor
C3, C4, C5, C6, C8 - .1 mf capacitor
C7 - 10 mf electrolytic capacitor
C9 - 100 mf electrolytic capacitor
IC1 - MM54104 Speech Processor IC
IC2 - MM52164SSR1 ROM IC
IC3* - MM52164SSR2 ROM IC (connected in series with IC2)
IC4 - LM741 Op Amp
IC5 - LM386 Low Voltage Audio Power Amplifier IC
M1 - 8-ohm speaker
R1, R3 - 1M resistor
R2 - 1.8K resistor
R4 - 3.3K resistor
R5 - 10K resistor
R6 - 10K potentiometer
R7 - 10-ohm resistor
S1 - SPDT momentary switch
S2, S3, S4, S5, S6, S7, S8, S9 - SPDT switch
X1 - 4.0 MHz crystal
```

quire the + 5 V can all draw their power directly from the + 5 V source.

Following standard speech synthesizer construction practices, first solder all of the IC sockets to the selected PC board. Pay careful attention to this placement, in order to prevent future component spacing problems. Next, beginning with the audio amplifier IC (LM386), solder all of the resistors and capacitors into place. You will also need to prepare four 6-8 inch lengths of wire for future connection to the 10K pot (2 pieces; one to pin 3 of the 386 and the other to ground), speaker ground, and speaker power. After you have completed the amplifier section, solder the filter's components starting from pin 39 of the MM54104 and working towards the final 6-8″ connection wire for the 10K pot. The last support component subsection that needs to be soldered into place is the oscillator. These two resistors, two capacitors, and single crystal are all connected between pins 1 and 2 of the MM54104.

A total of 8 SPDT switches are connected to pins 8-15 of the MM54104 at their central posts. Each of the other switch posts are connected to the 7-11 V power source and ground, respectively. Another SPDT switch, this one a spring return momentary version, is placed between this power/ground combination and the Write Strobe pin (pin 4)

of the MM54104. The addition of a 1M power resistor to this pin enables an on-board key debounce circuit. Successful analog switch operation is dependent on this feature.

Once all of the support components have been added and the switches
are installed, the DT1050 address and data wiring is completed. Each
wire length should be kept to an absolute minimum. This will prevent
interference from distorting the data flow. Due to the series connection
between the two 64K bit ROMs, a certain degree of wiring difficulty will
be encountered. Different colored wires for the address and data lines
will make identification of this "spaghetti" much easier. All 24 pins from
each of the ROMs must be wired, pin-for-pin, to each other. These joint
connections are then soldered to their required power, ground, and
MM54104 pins.

An area that merits some serious thought is the nature of the power
source. The Phrase Maker uses both +5 V and +7-11 V as its power
supply. Basically, you have two avenues for meeting these power needs.
First, you can use two sets of battery packs. One pack will supply the
+5 V and the other will produce +9 V (the mid value in the +7-11 V
range). Unless you have stock in a battery company, this solution might
prove undesirable. The high current drain that is generated by The Phrase
Maker will limit the life of these battery packs. An SPST power switch,
however, will help alleviate a better portion of this power drain.

The second solution to this dual power supply dilemma is to use external line voltage. As a rule, designing your own internally mounted
power regulator circuit creates nothing but troubles; namely an overabun-
dance of heat and a bulky container. A better answer is to use one of
the commercially available power adapters, similar to those used by many
computer peripherals. Depending on the voltage generated by this
adapter, a regulator IC (e.g., 7805) will have to be used to trim the power
down to the +9 V and +5 V requirements. For example, with a +12
V power adapter, one 7805, with the proper support components, would
reduce the voltage to +9 V. By using another properly equipped 7805
in series with the first 7805, a final voltage of +5 V can be drawn. This
arrangement would supply all of the voltages that are required by The
Phrase Maker.

OPERATION OF THE PHRASE MAKER

There are a total of 144 different words, sounds, and pauses contained on the DT1050 ROM chip set (see Table 4-2). The initial test for
ensuring the proper construction of The Phrase Maker is to place *all* of
the 8 SPDT data bit switches in the down or "off" position (this is assuming that you have wired each of these switches in a standard configuration). Then the momentary SPDT is used to pulse the Write Strobe
pin. If everything has been properly assembled, you will hear The Phrase

Table 4-2. The ROM Vocabulary and Their
Decimal Addresses of the DT1050 IC Set.

Decimal Address	Word
0	This is Digitalker
1	One
2	Two
3	Three
4	Four
5	Five
6	Six
7	Seven
8	Eight
9	Nine
10	Ten
11	Eleven
12	Twelve
13	Thirteen
14	Fourteen
15	Fifteen
16	Sixteen
17	Seventeen
18	Eighteen
19	Nineteen
20	Twenty
21	Thirty
22	Forty
23	Fifty
24	Sixty
25	Seventy
26	Eighty
27	Ninety
28	Hundred
29	Thousand
30	Million
31	Zero
32	A
33	B
34	C
35	D
36	E
37	F
38	G

Decimal Address	Word
39	H
40	I
41	J
42	K
43	L
44	M
45	N
46	O
47	P
48	Q
49	R
50	S
51	T
52	U
53	V
54	W
55	X
56	Y
57	Z
58	Again
59	Ampere
60	And
61	At
62	Cancel
63	Case
64	Cent
65	A musical tone
66	A musical tone
67	Pause
68	Pause
69	Pause
70	Pause
71	Pause
72	Centi
73	Check
74	Comma
75	Control
76	Danger
77	Degree
78	Dollar
79	Down
80	Equal

Decimal Address	Word
81	Error
82	Feet
83	Flow
84	Fuel
85	Gallon
86	Go
87	Gram
88	Great
89	Greater
90	Have
91	High
92	Higher
93	Hour
94	In
95	Inches
96	Is
97	It
98	Kilo
99	Left
100	Less
101	Lesser
102	Limit
103	Low
104	Lower
105	Mark
106	Meter
107	Mile
108	Milli
109	Minus
110	Minute
111	Near
112	Number
113	Of
114	Off
115	On
116	Out
117	Over
118	Parenthesis
119	Percent
120	Please
121	Plus
122	Point

Decimal Address	Word
123	Pound
124	Pulses
125	Rate
126	Re
127	Ready
128	Right
129	SS (plurals)
130	Second
131	Set
132	Space
133	Speed
134	Star
135	Start
136	Stop
137	Than
138	The
139	Time
140	Try
141	Up
142	Volt
143	Weight

Maker say, "This is Digitalker."

Trying to identify each of the eight data bit switches can be a difficult proposition. The best solution is to place the switch that is connected to pin 8 (the MSB) of the MM54104 on the far left of your selected container. Each subsequent switch from pin 9 through 15 (the LSB) is positioned, in a linear fashion, to the right of the pin 8 switch. For the sake of convenience, label each of these switches 1-8 starting with the left switch. Your container should now have eight SPDT switches labeled: 1, 2, 3, 4, 5, 6, 7, and 8. Now each ROM address in The Phrase Maker can be identified by a series of switch labels. For example, 2-5-6 indicates that only switches 2, 5, and 6 should be placed in the "on" position. Furthermore, this example can then be represented as a binary value,

01001100

where, a 1 signifies a switch in the "on" position.

One final caution, switch settings which exceed the 144 different ROM address points will produce random sounds and noises. In other words, addresses above the setting 1-5-6-7-8 (or 10001111 binary) enter the world of undocumented DT1050 terrain. Many of you sharper eyed readers will have noticed that this binary value equals 143 and you are probably wondering what happened to the 144th address. Actually, you were introduced to this address when you tested The Phrase Maker. The switch setting 00000000 (binary value) is our first true address. Therefore, 0-143 equals a total of 144 different ROM addresses.

APPLICATIONS FOR THE PHRASE MAKER

The Phrase Maker is the ideal instructional tool for students at various levels of education. At a beginning level, the student could practice both the correct vocal formation and the proper sequence for the alphabet and numbers 0-20. An easy to understand switch toggling scheme will move any student quickly through a lesson in the number system (binary values 00000001-00010100). Additionally, this same type of switch flipping will cover all of the letters from A to Z (binary values 00100000-00111001).

Slightly more advanced students will profit from The Phrase Maker's ability to form elementary sentences. In fact, one instructor used The Phrase Maker in her English classroom as a unique demonstration of an artificial vocal mechanism. In this experimental situation, the student could only use The Phrase Maker for speaking to the class. This instructor's results indicated that each student developed a rapport with The Phrase Maker and learned to become a more effective communicator. Whether this care and concern transcended the confines of the classroom remains to be documented. Even practice with plurals is possible by adding the stored word "ss" (switch setting 1-8) to the end of different words. Finally, the nature of the formation of the binary values for each of ROM addresses can be used in the mathematics classroom.

ONE MORE STEP

A new set of ROM chips is available for external processing through the MM54104. This two chip set, called DT1057, expands the 144 word and sound vocabulary of the original DT1050 up to 250 different words. The special addressing limits of 128K bits ROM can be overcome in the DT1050 system through external expansion. Complete expansion techniques are provided with the DT1057 chip set. Who knows, if you fail to follow the prescribed expansion procedures, you might hear: /01000010/ /10001010/ /01100110/ /01100000/ /01101111/.

Section II

Computer-Based
Speech Synthesizers

IF YOU ARE AFTER THE GREATEST DEGREE OF REALISM IN SPEECH
synthesis, then you will need a microcomputer to make your synthesizer twist its tongue. Basically, the microcomputer is able to flip the digital equivalent of the analog switches that are found in stand-alone speech synthesizers with greater speed and accuracy. Additionally, the computer is able to control the sophisticated speech attributes that are present in most of today's speech synthesis ICs. These parameters include: phoneme duration, inflection, and pitch. While the control of these attributes eluded us in the stand-alone designs, they are only a POKE away with computer-based speech synthesizers.

A major thorn in the side of computer-based speech synthesizer design is in deciding which computer model to center the circuit around. Based on a current sampling of the most popular microcomputers, the most dominant are the Apple *II*e, the Commodore 64, and the IBM PC. Therefore, special construction considerations have been given to owners of these computers. Other computer model owners don't need to fret. The majority of the designs in this section are made for either an RS-232C port or a Centronics parallel port interface. This means that each owner will only have to create his or her own software. How's that for a virtually universal speech synthesis design?

There are two different types of computer-based speech synthesizers that are presented in this section: internal and external. The internal speech synthesizer is usually contained on an expansion card that mounts inside the computer's main CPU housing (see Fig. II-1). The exception to this rule is the Commodore 64 which uses an external expansion slot. For all intents and purposes, however, this external port is classified as an internal expansion slot. Two of the primary advantages of the internal speech synthesizer are an access to a power supply and the elimination of desktop clutter. Neither of these points should be taken lightly. An internal power supply greatly simplifies the speech synthesizer's design. Furthermore, there is no need to attach yet another external power supply to your already dwindling number of household power outlets. Finally, the elimination of desktop clutter means that the internal speech synthesizer is out-of-sight, tucked away inside the computer. Lying in a dormant state, this circuit is always ready for your summons through a software call.

The external speech synthesizer, on the other hand, beats the top complaint against the internal speech synthesizer—restricted design. In simple terms, once you build an internal speech synthesizer for a specific computer model, *that* circuit is restricted to *that* computer for its lifetime. In other words, the internal design offers very little "brand name"

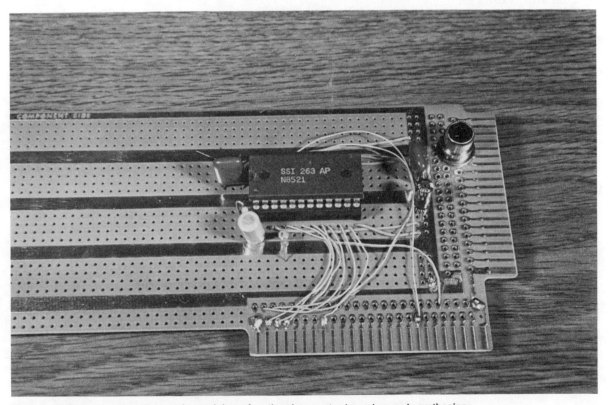

Fig. II-1. An Apple *IIe* expansion card containing a functional computer-based speech synthesizer.

interchange. External speech synthesizers are made to operate through common, external computer ports. The two most common of these interface points are: the RS-232C serial port and the Centronics parallel port. Unfortunately, even these industry standards suffer from a variety of different manufacturer interpreted alterations. In order to minimize any potential conflict from these variants, each of the external speech synthesizer projects in this section adhere to the commonly accepted pinouts for these two ports.

There are five computer-based projects in this section. Each project is based on a different speech synthesis IC. The first project uses the ubiquitous Votrax SC-01 (Chapter 5). This project, known as The Phoneme Synthesizer, is an external design that connects to any Centronics parallel port. Another phoneme synthesizer project, The Advanced Phoneme Synthesizer (Chapter 6), operates on the expanded capabilities of the Silicon Systems SSI 263A IC. In order to contrast the differences between external and internal designs, The Advanced Phoneme Synthesizer is an internal computer-based speech synthesizer. Provisions have been made in this chapter to accommodate Apple *II*e, Commodore 64, and IBM PC owners.

A more advanced speech synthesis project, that links the GI SPO256-AL2 with the GI CTS 256-AL2, is The Text-to-speech Synthesizer (Chapter 7). This external speech synthesizer project interfaces with the RS-232C port of virtually any microcomputer. The correct functioning of this project is dependent on the reader's ability to send true ASCII text files to The Text-to-speech Synthesizer through an RS-232C port under a rigid set of transmission parameters. Don't give up yet; several simple hardware techniques are suggested for achieving this goal.

The ROM Synthesizer (Chapter 8) is an external, computer-based alternative to the DT1050 stand-alone project (see Chapter 4). By using the Texas Instruments TMS5110A IC and the TI VM61006A ROM IC, a 198 word vocabulary is directly accessible through an interface port of your choice. It is even possible, through a little experimentation, to program your own EPROM with words of your creation.

The last project in this section is the most complex, as well as the most intelligible. The ADPCM Synthesizer uses the Oki Semiconductor MSM5218RS IC (Chapter 9). This unique chip is able to analyze human speech input, store it, and synthesize its output. The result is a speech synthesizer that shares virtually the same vocal attributes as the speaker. The open nature of this project makes it adaptable to virtually any computer model. Therefore, its construction strays from the internal and external definitions provided earlier. All you will need is the right interface for your computer and a piece of software to control the circuit. All in all, this is a speech synthesizer that you can truly sample and hold.

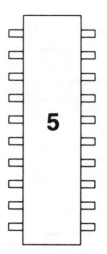

5

Votrax SC-01

A S WAS POINTED OUT IN CHAPTER 1, THE BASIC BUILDING BLOCK of speech is the phoneme. Multiples of these elemental speech units are combined in varying patterns and form the enormous variety of spoken words and sounds that the human being is capable of producing. But the assignment of phonemes to the written word can be a difficult one. For example, the *e* in "bed" sounds different from the *e* in "racket." Therefore, two phonemes are necessary for distinguishing between these similar spellings that have different sounds.

For the most part, this diversity in sound for identical spellings results in a large phoneme list. The average speech synthesizer uses 59-63 phonemes (this number increases to 64 phonemes, if you count pauses and stops) to duplicate the varied sounds of human speech. With such a large number of different sounds to address and manipulate, true and accurate speech synthesis is only possible when operated under the control of a microprocessor.

The actual synthesis of these phonemes is most commonly accomplished through formant synthesis and, more specifically, phoneme synthesis. This electronic simulation of the human vocal mechanism uses frequencies produced by a series of filters to encode a phoneme (see Chapter 2). Each phoneme is assigned a unique address that can be directly accessed through a data bus. Once this address value is selected, the synthesis circuit reproduces the assigned frequencies that represent the phoneme. The result is a spoken phoneme for each address input. Carrying this example even further, with just a modest amount of microprocessor support, strings of these phoneme addresses can be tied together and words, phrases, and sentences will be uttered.

THE VOTRAX SC-01

The Votrax SC-01 is a CMOS (complementary metal oxide semiconductor) LSI IC (see Fig. 5-1). The employment of CMOS technology makes the SC-01 have a nominal current drain of 9 mA, tolerate a broad power supply range (9-14 V), and offer a high input impedance. Eight different data input lines are used for controlling the phoneme construction algorithm which, in turn, stimulates the frequency generating filters found inside the SC-01's vocal mechanism simulation.

A total of 64 different phonemes (which includes two pauses and one stop) are addressed through a 6-bit input code that is automatically latched. Furthermore, a 2-bit input code is used for pitch assignments. The phoneme data input lines are 5 V TTL (transistor-transistor logic) compatible, while the pitch lines need external latches and an input volt-

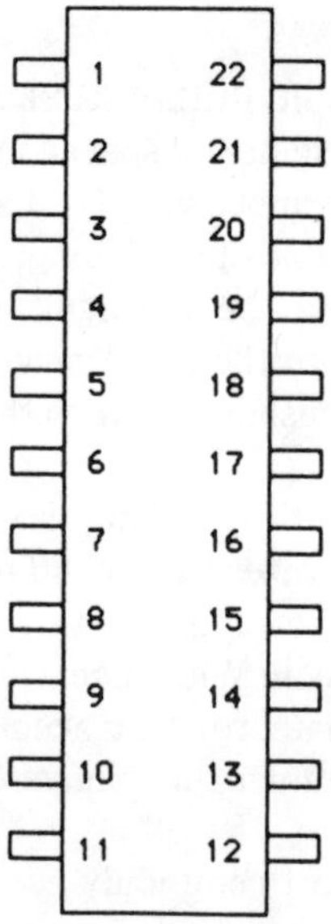

Pin Assignments			
Pin Number	Function	Pin Number	Function
1	V_P	12	P2
2	I2	13	P1
3	I1	14	P0
4	NC	15	MCX
5	TP3	16	MCRC
6	TP2	17	TP1
7	STB	18	V_G
8	A/R	19	NC
9	P5	20	CB
10	P4	21	AF
11	P3	22	A0

Fig. 5-1. Pin assignments for SC-01.

age that matches the SC-01's power supply. The 6-bit phoneme data input is latched when the Strobe pin (STB; pin 7) is pulsed from a low logic to a high state. Receipt of the phoneme data is acknowledged by a logic 1 to a logic 0 change on the Acknowledge/Request pin (AR; pin 8). A data bit rate of 70 bps is required for producing this phoneme speech. The 2-bit pitch lines are used for the instantaneous setting of the speech's inflection. Finally, phoneme duration is controlled by the resistor and capacitor values attached to the Master Clock Resistor-Capacitor pin (MCRC; pin 16).

CONSTRUCTION OF THE PHONEME SYNTHESIZER

The Phoneme Synthesizer uses a total of four ICs (see Fig. 5-2 and Table 5-1). Two of these ICs are used for buffering the parallel data input (74LS244) and shifting the voltage level to the TTL requirements of the SC-01 (7416). In addition to the SC-01 IC, the final IC is an audio amplifier (LM386). This amp is connected to a low-pass filter and drives an 8-ohm speaker.

The low pin number of these ICs makes The Phoneme Synthesizer occupy very little PC board space. Special consideration must be given, however, to the size and location of the parallel jack that is a part of this circuit. Therefore, a 4 × 5″ PC board is the best candidate for this project (e.g., Radio Shack #276-187). Two additional PC board features that will be beneficial in the later construction steps are a set of dual bus strips, one for power (either +5 V or +12 V) and another for ground, and a provision for the addition of a parallel port (only 10 of the possible 36 Centronics parallel connections will be used).

Begin the construction of The Phoneme Synthesizer by soldering the IC sockets into place. Be sure to allow yourself plenty of space for the addition of the support components and the connection wiring. You are now ready to add the resistors and capacitors that constitute the low-pass filter and audio amplifier section. Wire lengths of 6-8″ should be used for the two speaker connections and the three 10K audio taper pot connections. The low-pass filter is tied to pins 20, 21, and 22 (CB, AF, AO, respectively) of the SC-01.

Before tackling the parallel port connections, two minor dual pin connections must be made. Since the pitch changes produced by the 2-bit inflection address are negligible, these two pins (I1; pin 3 and I2; pin 2) are tied to ground. The second dual pin connection is the frequency adjust between MCX (pin 15) and MCRC (pin 16). The 50K pot used in this connection can be either an internal PC board mount or an external audio taper. This choice is hinged on whether you will want to make frequent changes to the frequency of output or set a fixed level. I prefer the variable nature of an external audio taper. Many interesting sound effects are made possible by sweeping this 50K pot during output. For

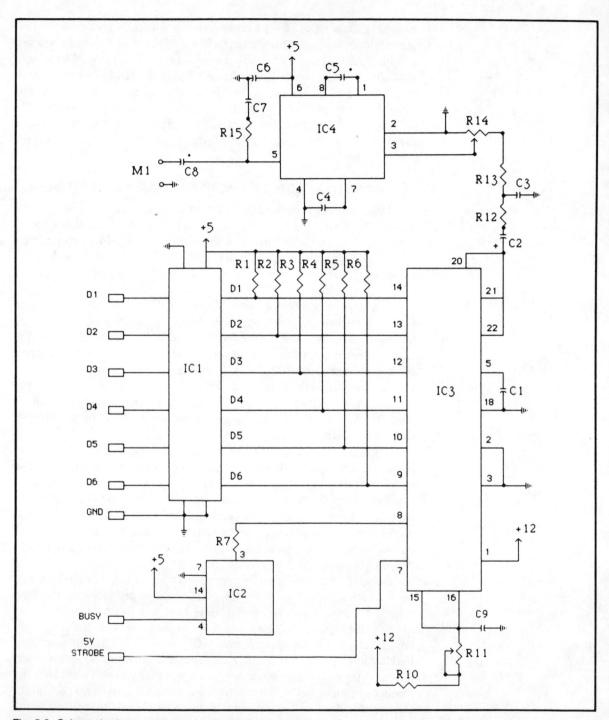

Fig. 5-2. Schematic diagram for The Phoneme Synthesizer.

Table 5-1. Parts List for The Phoneme Synthesizer.

C1 – .01 mf capacitor
C2 – 4.7 mf electrolytic capacitor
C3 – .047 mf capacitor
C4, C6, C7 – .1 mf capacitor
C5 – 10 mf electrolytic capacitor
C8 – 100 mf electrolytic capacitor
C9 – 100 pf capacitor
IC1 – Line Buffer IC; e.g. 74LS244 Octal Buffer/Line Driver/Line Receiver or 7417 IC
IC2 – Inverter Buffer IC; e.g. 4049 or 7416 Hex Inverter Buffer/Driver IC
IC3 – SC-01 CMOS Phoneme Speech Synthesizer IC
IC4 – LM386 Low Voltage Audio Power Amplifier IC
M1 – 8-ohm speaker
R1, R2, R3, R4, R5, R6, R12 – 4.7K resistor
R7 – 39K resistor
R10 – 6.8K resistor
R11 – 50K potentiometer
R13 – 10K resistor
R14 – 10K potentiometer
R15 – 10-ohm resistor

speech purists, however, this pot can be set and forgotten.

The last major assembly point in the construction of The Phoneme Synthesizer is the parallel port. Seven of the ten pins used in the parallel port are connected to the 74LS244 buffering IC. The other three pins are used for latching the phoneme data bit input. All of the pin assignments in this parallel port follow the standard Centronics parallel port configuration. One requirement that is absolutely necessary for this interface to function properly is the pulse duration on the Data Strobe pin (on the computer's Centronics port). This pulse must have a duration of a minimum of 100 microseconds for proper operation. If your computer lacks the proper pulse timing, a pulse extender can be inserted between the Data Strobe pin of the computer's Centronics port and the Strobe pin of The Phoneme Synthesizer. A monostable multivibrator IC (e.g., 74121) is the basis for this pulse extender.

Finally, the odd power requirements of this circuit might present a problem during the final assembly stages. The ideal power supply would be a dual voltage (+5 V and +12 V), external adapter akin to those found with many computer peripherals. This type of power source would require no further modifications for its incorporation into this project. Alternatively, a single voltage (+ 12 V), external power adapter could also be used. A power regulator IC attached to the main voltage line from this adapter would reduce the + 12 V to a + 5 V level. An example of this type of power source is illustrated in Fig. 5-3.

OPERATION OF THE PHONEME SYNTHESIZER

When The Phoneme Synthesizer is connected to your computer via its Centronics parallel port, simple BASIC LPRINT statements are all that are necessary for addressing phonemes. Of course, computers like the Apple *IIe* and the Commodore 64 will require a slightly different programming approach. Use the following programming example to test your completed project:

10 LPRINT "[B#X#57";"?"

In Applesoft BASIC, this same test is:

Fig. 5-3. This surplus four-output power supply can satisfy all of The Phoneme Synthesizer's power needs.

```
10 PRINT CHR$(4)
20 PR# 1
30 PRINT "[B#X#57";"?";
40 PRINT CHR$(4);
50 PR# 0
```

In Commodore BASIC, this same test is:

```
10 OPEN 4,4,4
20 PRINT#4,"[B#X#57";"?";
30 CLOSE4
```

The strange ASCII characters inside each of these PRINT statements (and the original LPRINT statement) are used to represent the SC-01 phonemes (see Table 5-2). Therefore, an alphanumeric character can be sent to the computer's parallel port and the hardware will handle the phoneme address conversion. This makes programming The Phoneme Synthesizer both quick and easy.

APPLICATIONS FOR THE PHONEME SYNTHESIZER

Two features of The Phoneme Synthesizer make it suitable for language instruction. First, the computer's microprocessor handles all of the individual phoneme stringing. This control can lead to the development of an extensive phoneme-constructed speech dictionary. In this way, students will be able to more fully appreciate the interrelationships between vowels and consonants. The second major advantage of The Phoneme Synthesizer is the use of the Centronics parallel port. By using this port, simple software drivers can be written in BASIC. In fact, a three line BASIC test program would be more than adequate for using The Phoneme Synthesizer in an introductory language laboratory.

As an example of a "real" application, a test version of The Phoneme Synthesizer was used by a college language instructor to illustrate phoneme relationships to his students. In this demonstration, phonemes were combined to form words with allophonic variations. The students in this class were then able to dissect each word in search of the specific allophones.

ONE MORE STEP

An exciting experiment that can be added to this basic SC-01 project is a custom speech dictionary. This dictionary would be stored as phoneme strings in an EPROM. Then when the data bit address is received from the parallel port, the EPROM intercepts the address, con-

Table 5-2. The Phonemes and Their Decimal Addresses of the SC-01 IC.

Decimal Address	Phoneme	Example
0	EH3	Racket
1	EH2	Enlist
2	EH1	Levy
3	PA0	Pause
4	DT	Flutter
5	A2	Raid
6	A1	Maid
7	ZH	Azure
8	AH2	Honest
9	I3	Inhibit
10	I2	Inhibit
11	I1	Inhibit
12	M	Mad
13	N	Bun
14	B	Bat
15	V	Vase
16	CH	Chop
17	SH	Shop
18	Z	Zebra
19	AW1	Raw
20	NG	Ring
21	AH1	Ought
22	OO1	Looking
23	OO	Book
24	L	Lose
25	K	Lick
26	J	Jury
27	H	Help
28	G	Good
29	F	Fun
30	D	Dead
31	S	Gas
32	A	Paid
33	AY	Lay
34	Y1	Year
35	UH3	Graduation
36	AH	Rot
37	P	Perfect
38	O	Sold

39	I	B<u>i</u>n
40	U	Gr<u>oo</u>ve
41	Y	Man<u>y</u>
42	T	<u>T</u>oo
43	R	<u>R</u>ead
44	E	B<u>ea</u>t
45	W	<u>W</u>onder
46	AE	M<u>a</u>d
47	AE1	<u>A</u>t
48	AW2	<u>A</u>ll
49	UH2	<u>A</u>bout
50	UH1	R<u>u</u>nt
51	UH	C<u>u</u>t
52	O2	<u>O</u>ar
53	O1	B<u>oa</u>rd
54	IU	D<u>ew</u>
55	U1	Y<u>ou</u>
56	THV	<u>Th</u>em
57	TH	<u>Th</u>in
58	ER	H<u>er</u>d
59	EH	B<u>e</u>t
60	E1	F<u>ee</u>
61	AW	B<u>a</u>ll
62	PA1	Pause
63	STOP	Pause

verts the value to the stored phoneme string, and sends this string to the SC-01 for processing. A special counter IC controls the addressing of the EPROM. This advancement would enlarge the number of applications that are possible with The Phoneme Maker. In fact,

```
(L)PRINT "2MXKLK*J^";"?";
(L)PRINT "__%<)*P";"?";
(L)PRINT "KIR";"?";"F!)";"?";
(L)PRINT "%U#__#NKIXKI*<!)" "?";
```

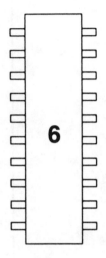

6

Silicon Systems SSI 263A

BY NOW, YOU SHOULD HAVE A PRETTY FAIR IDEA OF THE STRUC-
ture of speech. The composition and arrangement of the elemental
phonemes form the basis of this understanding (please refer to Chapter
1, if any of this discussion sounds alien to you). Furthermore, the differen-
tiation between phonemes, allophones, and pauses contribute to the
production of speech. A person who can master all of these individual
speech parts and exercise complete control over their numerous rule
parameters is considered to possess a fluency in speech. This same lofty
goal is highly sought in speech synthesis.

If you are striving for fluency in a speech synthesizer, one of the more
unlikely synthesis methods to employ in this quest would be formant synthesis. Chapter 2 covers many of the reasons for avoiding formant and
phoneme synthesis, but fails to present an alternate case for support.
Theoretically, phoneme (or formant) synthesis would have application
in the production of highly intelligible speech, if the synthesizer could
handle a high data bit rate and also address multiple bytes of phoneme
data. Additionally, this chip would have to be receptive to an enhanced
level of programming. This software control must also be able to manipulate the phoneme's duration, inflection, and frequency. Actually, this theory is implemented in the Silicon Systems SSI 263A.

THE SILICON SYSTEMS SSI 263A

The Silicon Systems SSI 263A is a compact CMOS LSI device that can be driven by a + 5 V power source (see Fig. 6-1). Its analog output must be run through a low-pass filter and then amplified by an audio amplifier prior to reaching an external speaker.

There are five 8-bit registers in the SSI 263A that control the speech rate, pitch, pitch movement rate, amplitude, rate of articulation, vocal tract filter frequency response, phoneme selection, and phoneme duration. All of these parameters are controlled via software. In each case, only eight data input lines (D0-pin 9, D1-pin 10, D2-pin 11, D3-pin 13, D4-pin 14, D5-pin 15, D6-pin 16, and D7-pin 17) are used for controlling each parameter. The status of these lines is determined by the logic of three register address pins (RS2-pin 6, RS1-pin 7, and RS0-pin 8). For example, when RS2, RS1, and RS0 all have a logic of 0, the 8 data lines are used for selecting both the phoneme and its duration. From this example, it is also possible to realize that the SSI 263A is capable of generating 256 different phonemes. In other words, 64 true phonemes, each with 4 different durations. Under all circumstances, D0 represents the LSB and D7 equals the MSB.

CONSTRUCTION OF THE ADVANCED PHONEME SYNTHESIZER

A fine tribute to the technicians at Silicon Systems is the complete absence of ancilliary support ICs from the design of The Advanced Phoneme Synthesizer. In fact, as described in this chapter, The Advanced Phoneme Synthesizer can be constructed from one SSI 263A and seven support components (see Fig. 6-2 and Table 6-1).

As a matter of convenience, you will need an Apple *II*e bus PC board for building The Advanced Phoneme Synthesizer (e.g., Vector Electronic Company #4609DP). Regardless of the brand of board that you use, there should be a 50-position edge connector along the long base of the board. This type of connector perfectly matches the specifications of the Apple *II*e internal expansion slots. Therefore, on completion, The Advanced Phoneme Synthesizer can be placed inside the Apple *II*e and directly addressed through software commands.

Begin your construction by soldering the 24-pin socket to the Apple *II*e bus board. In the case of the Vector board, this socket will be parallel to the 50-position edge connector. Follow the placement of the socket with the soldering of the seven support resistors and capacitors. The lion's share of the remaining work will consist of point-to-point wiring. Any 30-gauge wire wrap wire (e.g., Radio Shack #278-50X) can be used for these connections. Be sure to double check the origin and destination of each wire piece prior to final soldering. The extra time spent at this step will minimize the possibility for a future, system damaging, error.

The final construction step involves the attachment of the external amplifier/speaker jack. This connector will have to match the type of cabling that you plan on using. In other words, if you attach a phono jack

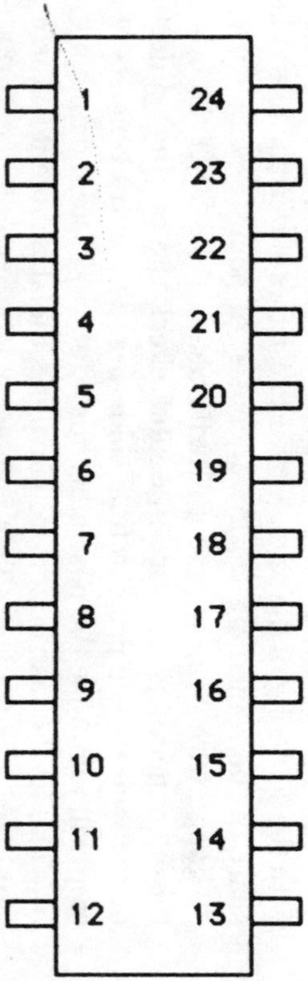

Pin Assignments

Pin Number	Function	Pin Number	Function
1	A0	13	D3
2	AGnd	14	D4
3	TP1	15	D5
4	A/$\overline{R}$	16	D6
5	TP2	17	D7
6	RS2	18	$\overline{PD}/\overline{RST}$
7	RS1	19	CS0
8	RS0	20	$\overline{CS1}$
9	D0	21	R/$\overline{W}$
10	D1	22	XCLK
11	D2	23	DIV2
12	DGnd	24	V_{ss}

Fig. 6-1. Pin assignments for SSI 263A.

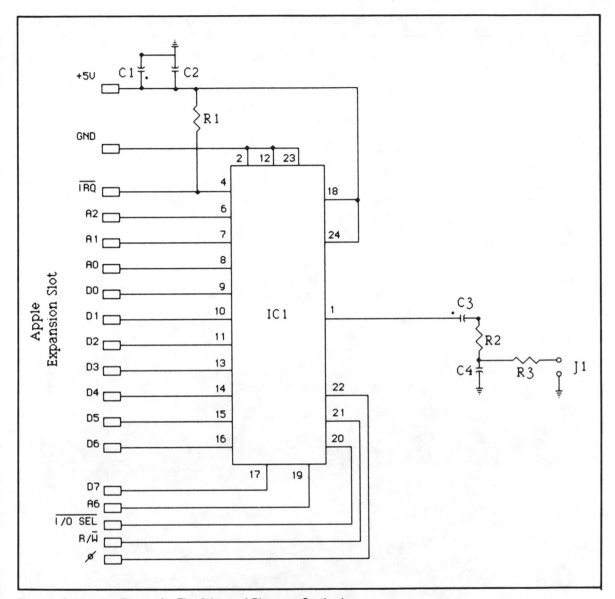

Fig. 6-2. Schematic diagram for The Advanced Phoneme Synthesizer.

you will need a cable with a phono plug on the end that will interface with The Advanced Phoneme Synthesizer. As a practical example, if you are going to use the built-in amplifier/speaker combination found in the Amdek Color-I composite monitor, then you will need a miniature phone jack (Radio Shack #274-251) for The Advanced Phoneme Synthesizer audio output. Installing this jack on the Vector PC board, for example,

Table 6-1. Parts List for The Advanced Phoneme Synthesizer.

```
C1, C3 - 10 mf electrolytic capacitor
C2 - .1 mf capacitor
C4 - .047 mf capacitor
IC1 - SSI 263A Phoneme Speech Synthesizer IC
J1 - phono jack (leading to an external amplifier &
     speaker)
R1 - 4.7K resistor
R2 - 2.2K resistor
R3 - 3.3K resistor
```

requires a 1/4″ hole. Careful selection of this hole's site will make grounding the jack a" snap" (see Fig. 6-3).

For those of you who would prefer to use the Apple *IIe*'s internal speaker, you will have to make two additions to the basic circuit presented in this chapter. First, you will need to add an on-board amplifier section.

Fig. 6-3. A dual-bus expansion card made grounding The Advanced Phoneme Synthesizer's output jack a snap.

This can consist of as little as seven extra components. An excellent choice for this amplifier section would be the 386 audio amplifier IC and its associated support pieces (please refer to one of the previous chapters for information on installing an LM386 IC). The second circuit addition is a special jack that will be used to connect the audio output from the 386 to the Apple's internal speaker. In this case, a 2-contact header jack (e.g., Radio Shack #276-1658) is soldered onto the Vector PC board. This two-pronged jack is then used to connect the Apple *II*e's speaker to The Advanced Phoneme Synthesizer.

OPERATION OF THE ADVANCED PHONEME SYNTHESIZER

The completed speech synthesizer card can be placed in any Apple *II*e slot except slot #3 and the auxiliary slot. These slots are reserved for special system expansion cards. You should be critical in determining your final slot destination, however. This selection will determine the nature of all of your future SSI 263A programming. Table 6-2 lists the addresses of each Apple *II*e expansion slot. In the following example, slot #4 will be used for illustrating the versatility of The Advanced Phoneme Synthesizer.

Several parameters of the SSI 263A must be set prior to sending a phoneme data string. These settings are used to control the input/output flow, phoneme duration, inflection, speech rate, amplitude, and filter frequency of the SSI 263A. The following program assumes a slot #4 location and instructs The Advanced Phoneme Synthesizer to speak its entire phonetic alphabet (see Table 6-3):

```
10   POKE 50243,255:REM Control Bit
20   POKE 50240,192:REM Duration
30   POKE 50241,63:REM Inflection
40   POKE 50242,160:REM Speech Rate
```

Table 6-2. The phonemes and Their Decimal Addresses of the SSI 263A IC.

Slot #	POKE Address
1	49408–49663
2	49664–49919
3	49920–50175
4	50176–50431
5	50432–50687
6	50688–50943
7	50944–51199

```
50   POKE 50243,120:REM Amplitude
60   POKE 50244,233:REM Filter Frequency
70   FOR X = 0 TO 63
80   POKE 50240,X:REM Speak Phoneme
90   FOR P = 1 TO 100:NEXT P
100  NEXT X
110  POKE 50240,0:REM Shut Up
120  END
```

In this example, there is extensive use of POKE statements. Each of these statements is necessary for addressing the internal registers and data lines of the SSI 263A. If any of these addresses are omitted from your programming, The Advanced Phoneme Synthesizer will utter nary a word. An important point to remember when programming the SSI 263A is that the last phoneme will be continually spoken unless it is stopped by a pause (PA). Line 110 in the above program makes sure that the last phoneme is properly silenced through a forced pause.

APPLICATIONS FOR THE ADVANCED PHONEME SYNTHESIZER

The ideal application for the SSI 263A is as a text-to-speech processor. Two companies already manufacture products that utilize this special ability (see Section III). Both of these commercial speech synthesizers have added a complex text-to-speech algorithm to the intelligible speech capabilities of the SSI 263A. Unfortunately, design differences preclude the possibility of combining this "canned" software with The Advanced Phoneme Synthesizer (although minor programming modifications will permit the Sweet Micro Systems software to work). Other applications are practical, however, with The Advanced Phoneme Synthesizer.

Through controlled usage of the special speech parameters that are inherent to the SSI 263A (inflection, duration, pitch, etc.), students can be introduced into the variability of "true" speech. This variation is especially true in foreign languages. By using the six special native foreign phonemes found in the SSI 263A, many French and German words can be synthesized. Therefore, the use of The Advanced Phoneme Synthesizer in the foreign language laboratory environment is a practical application for this versatile speech chip.

ONE MORE STEP

Owners of Commodore 64 and IBM PC computers can also share in the excitement of the SSI 263A IC by modifying The Advanced Phoneme Synthesizer to their computer's expansion slot requirements. You should be warned beforehand, however, that you will need to fully understand the identification and function of each pinout on your computer's

Table 6-3. The Phonemes of the SSI263A.

Decimal Address	Phoneme	Example
0	PA	Pause
1	E	Beat
2	E1	Rent
3	Y	He
4	YI	Yes
5	AY	Please
6	IE	Many
7	I	Bit
8	A	Raid
9	AI	Hare
10	EH	Bet
11	EH1	Help
12	AE	Mad
13	AE1	After
14	AH	Rot
15	AH1	Father
16	AW	Ought
17	O	Gore
18	OU	Rope
19	OO	Book
20	IU	Who
21	IU1	Hood
22	U	Ruin
23	U1	Lagoon
24	UH	One
25	UH1	Love
26	UH2	What
27	UH3	Hut
28	ER	Her
29	R	Root
30	R1	Rug
31	R2	-er (German)
32	L	Leaf
33	L1	Lay
34	LF	Ball (Final)
35	W	Wonder
36	B	Bug
37	D	Laid
38	KV	Rag (Glottal Stop)

Decimal Address	Phoneme	Example
39	P	Penny
40	T	Start
41	K	Kitchen
42	HV	(Hold Vocal)
43	HVC	(Hold Vocal Closure)
44	HF	Hear
45	HFC	(Hold Fricative Closure)
46	HN	(Hold Nasal)
47	Z	Zebra
48	S	Sum
49	J	Measure
50	SCH	Ship
51	V	Victory
52	F	Fun
53	THV	Them
54	TH	Both
55	M	Money
56	N	None
57	NG	Thing
58	:A	-a- (German)
59	:OH	-o- (French)
60	:U	-u- (German)
61	:UH	-u (French)
62	E2	-e (German)
63	LB	Lose

expansion slot, in order to make this modification successful. Additionally, you will need to be able to program the required POKE addresses for the register and data lines of the SSI 263A.

Connecting The Advanced Phoneme Synthesizer to the Commodore 64 computer's expansion port is the easiest of these two conversions. This interfacing is simplified by the similar microprocessors found in the Apple *II*e (6502) and the Commodore 64 (6510). Basically, all of the pin connections from the Apple version are duplicated on the Commodore 64 version. For example, the Apple's R/W connection (edge connector position 18) corresponds to the Commodore's R/W connection (edge connector position 5). Your only difficulty might be in finding the proper Commodore equivalent for Apple's I/O SEL connector. In this case, use Commodore's position 7 (I/O1) connector. After you have made your Commodore 64 Advanced Phoneme Synthesizer, you will have to convert the test program in the "Operation of The Advanced Phoneme Synthesizer" Section to the Commodore 64's addresses.

Making an IBM PC version of The Advanced Phoneme Synthesizer is complicated by the different data/address I/O structure of the 8088 microprocessor. For the most part, the data and address lines will make direct translations (e.g., Apple's position 42; D7 is equal to IBM's position A02; SYSDAT7). You will need to find suitable equivalents for the Apple's IRQ, A6, R/W, I/O SEL, and ϕ. As a beginning point you can try IBM's IRQST2 (position B04), SYSA6 (position A25), SYSIORD (position B14), and IOCHLRDY/WAIT (position A10) for the Apple IRQ, A6, R/W, and I/O SEL, respectively. IBM's clock frequency for the Apple ϕ connector will have to be acquired from a division of the 14.31818 MHz frequency of BSYSCLK1 (position B30). A 3.58 MHz color-burst signal is the desired result. Finally, you will have to make modifications to the test program which will accommodate the new POKE addresses of the IBM's expansion slot. No matter which version of The Advanced Phoneme Synthesizer that you make, you will find working with the SSI 263A to be as   /AY/ /Z/ /IE/ /PA/ /AE/ /Z/ /PA/ /P/ /AH/ /E/ /PA/.

7 General Instrument CTS256A-AL2

PHONEME AND ALLOPHONE STRING PROCESSING ARE ADEQUATE techniques for limited speech synthesis, but impractical for major text reading chores. For example, all of the previous speech synthesizer projects require the input of a string of phoneme data codes for each spoken word, phrase, and sentence. This procedure becomes increasingly tedious as the volume of text is raised. For every word that is to be synthesized, a phoneme must first be selected for representing each of the word's unique sounds. This string of phonemes must then be converted into an appropriate data string for transmission to the synthesizer's data input port. Finally, the converted string of phoneme data is sent to the synthesizer and the word is spoken.

Granted, you can save yourself some of this "brute force" labor by performing this translation under software control, but the size and speed of execution of this type of program would be prohibitive. Luckily, several dedicated researchers at the Naval Research Laboratories answered the need for this conversion program. In 1976, scientists Elovitz, Johnson, McHugh, and Shore, developed a small and compact algorithm that handled all of the analyzing and translation duties that are normally associated with converting a written word into a synthesized word. The elegant nature of this text-to-speech algorithm has made it the most popular method for converting ASCII text into synthesized speech. Only minor phonetic data structure alterations are necessary before this algorithm can be used with any speech synthesizer IC.

THE GENERAL INSTRUMENT CTS256A-AL2

The General Instrument CTS256A-AL2 is an NMOS LSI device with a 4.5-5.5 V operating voltage tolerance (see Fig. 7-1). There are two key features present in the CTS256A-AL2. First, this IC is actually an 8-bit

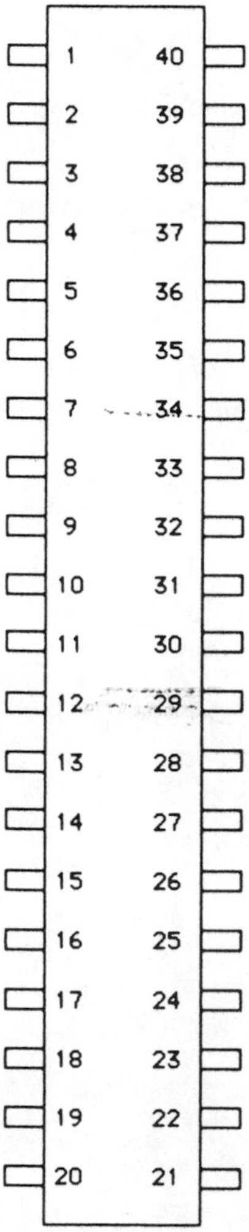

Pin Assignments			
Pin Number	Function	Pin Number	Function
1	B5/R/W	21	D5
2	B7/CLK OUT	22	D4
3	B0	23	D3
4	B1	24	D2
5	B2	25	V_{CC}
6	A0	26	D1
7	A1	27	D0
8	A2	28	C0
9	A3	29	C1
10	A4	30	C2
11	A7	31	C3
12	INT3	32	C4
13	INT1	33	C5
14	RESET	34	C6
15	A6/SCLK	35	C7
16	A5/RXD	36	MC
17	XTAL2/CLK IN	37	B3/TXD
18	XTAL1	38	B4/Latch
19	D7	39	B6/Enable
20	D6	40	V_{SS}

Fig. 7-1. Pin assignments for CTS256A-AL2.

microprocessor that is pin-compatible with the PIC7041 (programmable interrupt controller) microprocessor. This microprocessor equivalence provides the CTS256A-AL2 with the ability to handle external program processing. Secondly, the CTS256A-AL2 contains an on-board text-to-speech algorithm which translates ASCII text into allophonic code strings. These allophonic code strings are specifically matched to the data input signals that are used by the SPO256-AL2 speech synthesizer IC. Therefore, tying the CTS256A-AL2 together with the SPO256-AL2 creates an inexpensive text-to-speech processing system.

A flexible data address bus on the CTS256A-AL2 can accept either serial TTL signals or 8-bit parallel signals. Both of these interface methods are complemented by full hardware and software handshaking control.

CONSTRUCTION OF THE TEXT-TO-SPEECH SYNTHESIZER

This circuit represents one of the more complicated construction projects that is described in this book. There are seven major ICs, two different clock crystals, and numerous support components that comprise the basic Text-to-speech Synthesizer (see Fig. 7-2 and Table 7-1). This parts count increases dramatically, however, if the optional RAM buffer, discussed in the "One More Step" section, is incorporated into the design. Therefore, the rule of thumb with this project is take your time and triple-check each connection prior to soldering.

Due to this large number of ICs, you will need a rather spacious PC board for holding this circuit. A minimum surface area of 36 sq. inches (e.g., Radio Shack #276-190) will be necessary for holding The Text-to-speech Synthesizer. After you have selected and cleaned your PC board, solder the IC sockets into their final positions. Be sure to leave adequate support component space around the CTS256A-AL2, SPO256-AL2, and LM386 sockets.

Starting with the filter/amplifier section, attach all of the resistors and capacitors that connect between pin 24 of the SPO256-AL2 and the amp's volume pot. This 10K pot can be either an internal PC mount-type or an external audio taper type. Your final selection of this pot should be based on your intended usage of the circuit (i.e., constant volume vs. variable volume). Follow the soldering of these five parts, with the attachment of all of the amp's associated components. Use 6-8" lengths of wire for the two speaker connections. Additionally, if you plan on using the external 10K audio taper, three more pieces of 6-8" wire will need to be attached to this section.

The bulk of the remaining work consists of soldering connection wire between the various pins of the ICs. Before you begin this wiring, however, there are three other subsections that should be completed first. The initial subsection consists of the two different clock crystals that

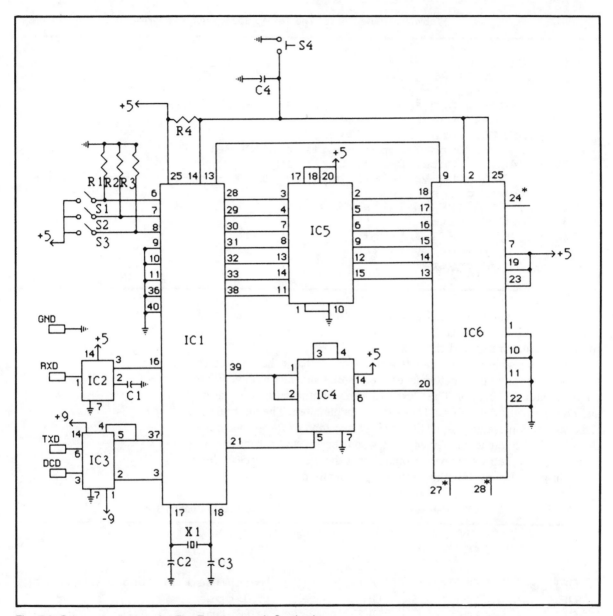

Fig. 7-2. Schematic diagram for The Text-to-speech Synthesizer.

must be attached to the CTS256A-AL2 and the SPO256-AL2. The 10 MHz crystal is connected between pins 17 and 18 of the CTS256A-AL2, while the 3.58 MHz crystal goes between pins 27 and 28 of the SPO256-AL2. The two other subsections are switches that reset the system and set the serial port parameters.

Table 7-1. Parts List for The Text-to-Speech Synthesizer.

```
C1 - 100 pf capacitor
C2, C3 - 47 pf capacitor
C4 - .1 mf capacitor
IC1 - CTS256A-AL2 Code-to-speech Processing Chip IC
IC2 - MC1489 Quad Line Receiver IC
IC3 - MC1488 Quad Line Driver IC
IC4 - 74LS00 Quad 2-input Positive-NAND Gate IC
IC5 - 74LS373 Octal D-type Latch IC
IC6 - SPO256-AL2 Voice Synthesizer IC (* - refer to Fig. 3-2 for
      these connections)
R1, R2, R3 - 10K resistor
R4 - 100K resistor
S1, S2, S3 - SPST switch
S4 - SPST momentary switch
X1 - 10 MHz crystal
```

The reset switch ties pins 2 and 25 of the SPO256-AL2 together with pin 14 of the CTS256A-AL2. Then, whenever this switch is activated, the hardware is reset and the system is initialized.

The other switch subsection is a three switch bank that is used to set the input mode parameters (see Table 7-2). Once again, depending on your intended use for The Text-to-speech Synthesizer, these three switches can be either internally or externally mounted. The internal variety would consist of a 4-position DIP switch (one of these four positions would be left unconnected) that would be set and forgotten. An externally mounted switch bank would permit the greatest degree of flexibility in your design. For this reason, I personally prefer a set of three

Table 7-2. Hardware Switch (S1-S3) Settings for The Text-to-Speech Synthesizer.

S1	S2	S3	Function
OFF	OFF	OFF	Not used in this circuit
OFF	OFF	ON	50 bps
OFF	ON	OFF	110 bps
OFF	ON	ON	300 bps
ON	OFF	OFF	1200 bps
ON	OFF	ON	2400 bps
ON	ON	OFF	4800 bps
ON	ON	ON	9600 bps

externally mounted SPST switches.

One final area that can be completed either before or after the pin-to-pin IC wiring is the installation of the RS-232C serial port. As a standard practice, this port should be a female DB-25 connector (e.g., Radio Shack #276-1548). All of the RS-232C connections are made to only three pins on the CTS256A-AL2, pins 3, 16, and 37 (the fourth connection is for a system ground). Your last construction step is to complete all of the wiring and mount the various subassemblies (PC board, battery pack, speaker, and switches) inside a suitable enclosure (e.g., Radio Shack #270-274).

OPERATION OF THE TEXT-TO-SPEECH SYNTHESIZER

After powering up The Text-to-speech Synthesizer, press the reset button to initialize the hardware system. If you have properly constructed this project, the circuit should answer with a verbal "O.K." following this system reset. You may now send standard ASCII text to this synthesizer for processing to produce speech.

In its present condition, The Text-to-speech Synthesizer is able to receive the following serial protocol: 7 bit word length, 2 stop bits, and no parity. Selective settings on the three-switch bank enable the various baud rates that the CTS256A-AL2 is able to use. A range of 50-9600 bps is possible. For most purposes, however, a baud rate of 1200 bps or less is ideal. If you find that you are experiencing data integrity troubles with The Text-to-speech Synthesizer, check that the communication parameters for both your computer and the circuit match. Many times a "bad circuit" fault can be traced to this innocent cause.

As it stands, The Text-to-speech Synthesizer lacks a large input buffer. This buffer is used for holding the ASCII codes that need to be converted and spoken. A total of 20 bytes will fit inside this input buffer at one time. Under optimal conditions, this represents a total of 19 "active" bytes plus a one byte delimiter. In the case of this circuit, this delimiter is represented by a carriage return character. Therefore, after a total of 19 bytes have been composed in the computer, they are followed by a delimiter. This 20 byte string is then sent to the synthesizer via the computer's RS-232C port. Unfortunately, by sending this maximum byte count, the result could be a total system "hang-up."

Even with handshaking, problems can occur in a full 20 byte transmission. This error is actually caused by the conversion of the ASCII text into its representative allophones and not by an input buffer overflow. In practice, the newly converted allophonic string is placed in an output storage buffer prior to sending it to the SPO256-AL2. This output buffer in the CTS256A-AL2 can hold a maximum of 26 bytes. Many times during this allophone conversion process two or more allophonic bytes are used to represent a single ASCII byte. Therefore, it's easy to see the kind of problems that can arise from an input of 19 active bytes. Basically, you will have an output buffer overflow and a system reset will be your only salvation.

One way to get around the possibility of an output buffer overflow is to limit the size of your ASCII text string. A safety margin of 10-15 text bytes (that's with the delimiter) will prove ample for reducing the chance of an output buffer overflow. If you find it impossible to deal with such a limited amount of text, read about the RAM buffer option in the "One More Step" section.

APPLICATIONS FOR THE TEXT-TO-SPEECH SYNTHESIZER

The most obvious application for The Text-to-speech Synthesizer is in "reading" text. This simple arrangement could be used as a reliable proofreader. Just input your text and listen to the spoken results. Many syntax errors that might otherwise escape your visual notice would be quickly picked up by your ear. Furthermore, you would have a chance to listen to your proposed speech and judge its overall audience acceptance value.

A local instructor carried this synthetic proofreading motif one step further. She used The Text-to-speech Synthesizer to introduce her pupils to proper spelling habits. In this case, each student was given a list of words to spell. This list was then read by the CTS256A-AL2. By listening to the results the students were then able to judge whether they had correctly or incorrectly matched the instructor's vocabulary list. Granted, this application isn't trying to exploit the full advantages of the computer/speech synthesizer combination, but it does provide each pupil with a generous degree of spelling practice.

As a sidelight to this classroom application, the real beauty in this example is that there was no need for any software or external programming control. A small portable computer (e.g., Radio Shack Model 100), operating in its text mode, was used for creating the vocabulary list. The student was then able to transmit this word file to The Text-to-speech Synthesizer by pressing one function key and entering a 5-digit number code. To the delight of the school administrator, this entire system cost less than one fifth the cost of a bare bones Apple *IIe* system. That's economy in education.

ONE MORE STEP

By adding just three additional ICs, the capacities of both the input and output buffers of The Text-to-speech Synthesizer can be increased (see Fig. 7-3 and Table 7-3). A single 2K × 8 RAM chip generates a 1792 byte input buffer and a 256 byte output buffer. Even with this larger buffer capacity you should still exercise some restraint in the exuberant

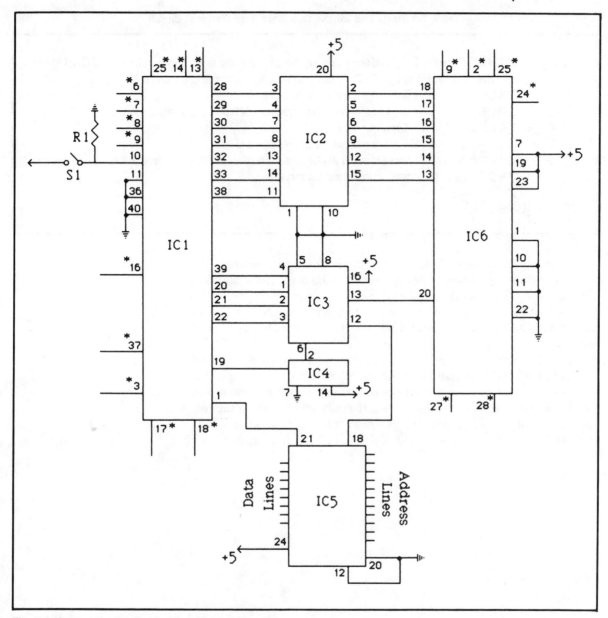

Fig. 7-3. Schematic diagram for One More Step.

input of lengthy ASCII text strings.

Both the B0 pin (pin 3) and the B3/TXD pin (pin 37) of the CTS256A-AL2 are used to control the flow of text into the input buffer. A BUSY signal (pin 3) and an XOFF signal (pin 37) are sent to the computer when the input buffer of The Text-to-speech Synthesizer becomes filled to

Table 7-3. Parts List for the One More Step Optional Circuit.

```
IC1  -  CTS256A-AL2 Code-to-speech Processing Chip IC (* -
         refer to Fig. 7-2 for these connections)
IC2  -  74LS373 Octal D-type Latch IC
IC3  -  74LS138 3-to-8 Line Decoder/Multiplexer IC
IC4  -  74LS04 Hex Inverter IC
IC5  -  6117 2K x 8-bit Static RAM IC
IC6  -  SP0256-AL2 Voice Synthesizer IC (* - refer to Fig.
         7-2 for these connections)
R1   -  10K resistor
S1   -  SPST switch
```

86.5% of capacity. Depending on the communication parameters of the computer, this signal can be either heeded or ignored. If the signal is ignored, the CTS256A-AL2 will execute an interrupt when the buffer reaches capacity. Finally, when the input buffer is reduced to 50% of capacity an XON signal is transmitted and the computer is free to send more text.

For all practical applications, The Text-to-speech Synthesizer should be made with this input/output buffer installed. It is far more logical to send several sentences or paragraphs of text for processing than it is to send isolated words or phrases. In fact, the only way to exploit the real advantages of The Text-to-speech Synthesizer is when it has been RAM powered.

8 Texas Instruments TMS5110A

THE TWO BASIC SPEECH SOUNDS, VOICED AND UNVOICED, THAT were discussed in Chapters 1 and 2, have a direct equivalence in electronics with periodic and random waveforms. These two waveforms when passed through a digital filter are then able to simulate the resonance and articulation qualities that are inherent to human speech. In this case, the periodic pulses of sound duplicates the vibrations of the human vocal cords and the white noise of the random waveform is similar to the hissing sounds found in fricatives. Once the proper sound source has been determined, it is passed through the digital filter. Actually, this digital filter is a series of filters that is each individually altered to match a specific frequency characteristic. This frequency enhanced change is then used to simulate the human vocal tract. Finally, the filter's output is converted to an analog output and sent to a suitable filter/amplifier circuit.

All of these actions translate into the LPC (linear predictive coding) speech synthesis method that was discussed in Chapter 2. With an LPC speech synthesizer, there are three different parameters that must be determined for each vocalization: sound source, pitch, and amplitude. As a rule, a 10-pole digital filter is the most common form of vocal tract simulation. Through the establishment of the various filter frequencies, an amplitude is set and the vocal tract is approximated. This final filter determination is later combined with the sound source and the sound source's pitch and sent to an A/D converter for production of the analog audio output. Only the truly dedicated LPC ICs contain all of these activities on-board. This is the working world of LPC speech synthesizers.

THE TEXAS INSTRUMENTS TMS5110A

The Texas Instruments TMS5110A is a PMOS (P-channel MOS) LSI package operating with a nominal (−8.3)-(−9.7 V) supply voltage range (see Fig. 8-1). An optimal data bit rate of 1200-1960 bps reproduces the highest quality of intelligible speech. Once the actual speech data string has been reconstructed through the digital filter series, an on-board 8-bit A/D converter and amplifier pull the signal up so that it can drive an 8-ohm speaker.

A 40 hertz input frame rate is standard on the TMS5110A. Conversely, the output speech waveform has an 8 kHz rate of change which

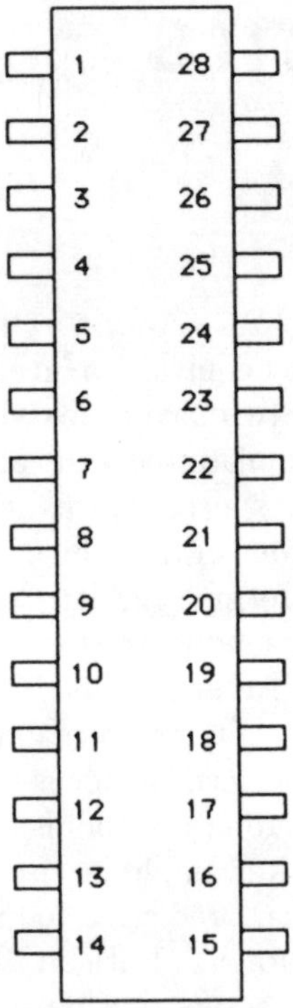

	Pin Assignments			
Pin Number	Function		Pin Number	Function
1	TST		15	MO
2	PDC		16	NC
3	ROM CLK		17	NC
4	CPU CLK		18	NC
5	V_{DD}		19	M1
6	NC		20	CTL4
7	RC OSC		21	ADD4
8	T11		22	ADD2
9	NC		23	CTL2
10	I/O		24	ADD1
11	SPK1		25	CTL1
12	SPK2		26	ADD8
13	PROM OUT		27	CTL8
14	V_{SS}		28	CS

Fig. 8-1. Pin assignments for TMS5110A.

equals a maximum speech output frequency of 4 kHz. Continuing from the input frame, this 49-bit frame shapes the filter parameters which are linearly interpolated every 3.12 ms and have a smooth waveform transition between each 25 ms frame interval. Therefore, the maximum 1960 bps data bit rate is arrived at for the highest possible speech intelligibility. Redundacy in waveform parameters will reduce this maximum bit rate to the lower 1200 bps limit.

A total of five pins control the loading and processing of data bit addresses. The actual data bit address lines (CTL8-pin 27, CTL4-pin 20, CTL2-pin 23, and CTL1-pin 25) also form the control bus. This control bus is used to both execute commands and to load data addresses. The standard protocol is transmission of the command followed by the transmission of the data. The fifth control pin is the processor data clock (PDC-pin 2). Pulsing this pin to a logic of 0 causes the current command or data bit address to be loaded. If a data bit address has been loaded into the TMS5110A, a Read Bit/Output command (100X) must follow this load prior to speaking. This "dummy read" is used to change the read flow of the ADD8 (pin 26) line from a processor output to a processor input.

CONSTRUCTION OF THE LPC SYNTHESIZER

A total of three ICs are used in the construction of The LPC Synthesizer (see Fig. 8-2 and Table 8-1). The two most important ICs, of course, are the TMS5110A and its associated ROM (VM61006A) (see Fig. 8-3). Both of these ICs, along with their single support IC, will easily fit on a PC board with 20 sq. inches of surface area (e.g., Radio Shack #276-187). The major bonus with the TMS5110A is its on-board filter and amplifier sections. Both of these features eliminate the need for an external low-pass filter and a LM386 audio amp IC. Just attach an 8-ohm speaker to pin 12 of the TMS5110A (SPK2) and The LPC Synthesizer will be heard.

In addition to the modest number of resistors, diodes, and capacitors, you will also need to locate a dual power supply that is capable of generating +5 V and −4.3 V. One method for producing the odd −4.3 V supply is through the regulation of a −12 V source. In this case, a −5 V regulator IC would be able to reduce the −12 V to an approximate −5 V level. Then by connecting a 1 amp rectifier diode to this −5 V output the desired −4.3 V supply can be generated.

One of the nice features of The LPC Synthesizer is that it is adaptable to many different computer expansion slots, as well as both parallel and serial interfaces. In other words, all you have to do is match your interface scheme to the five TMS5110A control lines. There is one point to remember during your interface construction, however. The TMS5110A has a supply voltage of −4.3 V. This voltage when added

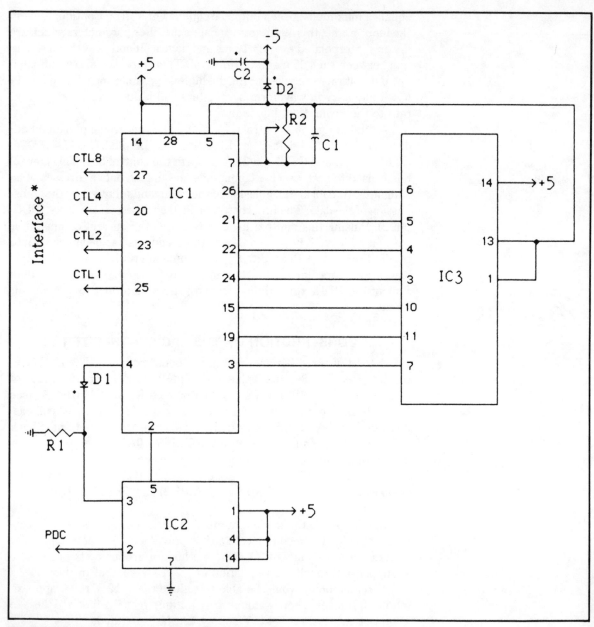

Fig. 8-2. Schematic diagram for The LPC Synthesizer.

to the Vss value (+5 V) produces the acceptable low logic signal level
for this synthesizer. Performing this addition gives a low logic value of
+.7 V. Therefore, make sure that your control line input signals are able
to properly present this low logic condition.

Table 8-1. Parts List for The LPC Synthesizer.

```
C1 - 47 pf capacitor
C2 - 100 mf electrolytic capacitor
D1 - 1N4149 Diode
D2 - 1N4002 Diode
IC1 - TMS5110A Voice Synthesis Processor IC
IC2 - 74LS74 Dual D-type Positive-edge-triggered Flip-
       flop IC
IC3 - VM61006A Voice Synthesis Memory IC
R1 - 1K resistor
R2 - 100K potentiometer
Interface* - provide the appropriate support components
             for your desired interface
```

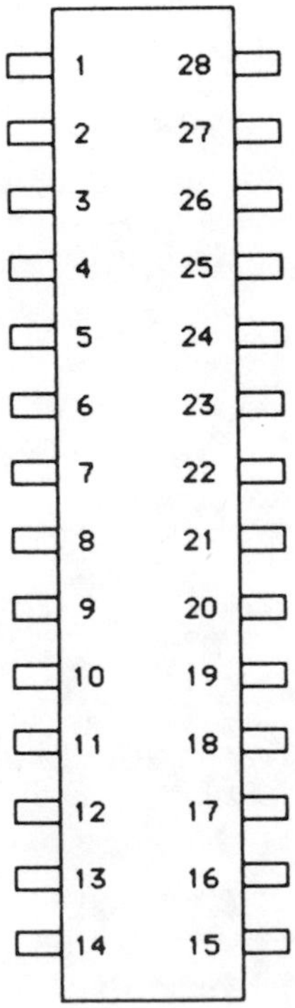

Pin Assignments			
Pin Number	Function	Pin Number	Function
1	V_{DD}	15	NC
2	NC	16	NC
3	DATA/ADD1	17	NC
4	DATA/ADD2	18	NC
5	DATA/ADD4	19	NC
6	DATA/ADD8	20	NC
7	CLK	21	NC
8	NC	22	NC
9	NC	23	NC
10	M0	24	NC
11	M1	25	NC
12	NC	26	NC
13	$\overline{CS}$	27	NC
14	V_{SS}	28	NC

Fig. 8-3. Pin assignments for VM61006A.

OPERATION OF THE LPC SYNTHESIZER

When you first turn on The LPC Synthesizer you might hear some random sounds. This occurrence is nothing to be concerned about. The actual programming is done in sequential data bit nibbles. This particular 4-bit code sequence is dictated by the use of a 4 data line address port on the TMS5110A. A typical sequence can consist of up to 12 separate numeric values.

For example, to make The LPC Synthesizer speak the word "yankee," the following code sequence would have to be sent to the TMS5110A:

2-C-2-8-2-0-2-0-2-0-C-A

[The hyphens are merely used as delimiters and should not be sent to the synthesizer.]

The individual elements of this code sequence are:

2- LOAD ADDRESS command
C800- VM61006A vocabulary code for "Yankee"
0- VM61006A ID code number
C- READ AND BRANCH command
A- SPEAK command

As a further explanation of the final code sequence, the LOAD ADDRESS command *must* precede each data bit entry whether the entry is either a command or speech data. Taking this rule one step further, when the 4-bit vocabulary code is being entered into the TMS5110A, a LOAD ADDRESS command is sent prior to each of these four data bits. Additionally, due to this address loading arrangement, the LSB must be sent first and the MSB sent last. Therefore, the code sequence portion:

2-C-2-8-2-0-2-0

represents the data for "yankee."

Three other parameters are sent after the speech data. These codes instruct the TMS5110A where to locate the vocabulary ROM (– 2-0), identify the speech data as a lookup table address (– C), and instruct the synthesizer to speak the data (– A). Only the ROM ID value must have the preceding LOAD ADDRESS command. Both the READ AND BRANCH and SPEAK codes are commands themselves and are able to be sent directly to the TMS5110A. As an aid in programming The LPC Synthesizer, all of the vocabulary addresses in Table 8-2 have already been converted into their LSB-to-MSB values. This means that all you will need to do to produce LPC speech is preface each data bit with a

Table 8-2. The ROM Vocabulary and
Their Hexadecimal Addresses of the TMS5110A IC Set.

Hex Address	Word
2-0-0-0	Zero
4-0-0-0	One
6-0-0-0	Two
8-0-0-0	Three
A-0-0-0	Four
C-0-0-0	Five
E-0-0-0	Six
0-1-0-0	Seven
2-1-0-0	Eight
4-1-0-0	Nine
6-1-0-0	Ten
8-1-0-0	Eleven
A-1-0-0	Twelve
C-1-0-0	Thir-
E-1-0-0	Fif-
0-2-0-0	-Teen
2-2-0-0	Twenty
4-2-0-0	Hundred
6-2-0-0	Thousand
8-2-0-0	A
A-2-0-0	B
C-2-0-0	C
E-2-0-0	D
0-3-0-0	E
2-3-0-0	F
4-3-0-0	G
6-3-0-0	H
8-3-0-0	I
A-3-0-0	J
C-3-0-0	K
E-3-0-0	L
0-4-0-0	M
2-4-0-0	N
4-4-0-0	O
6-4-0-0	P
8-4-0-0	Q
A-4-0-0	R
C-4-0-0	S
E-4-0-0	T

Hex Address	Word
0-5-0-0	U
2-5-0-0	V
4-5-0-0	W
6-5-0-0	X
8-5-0-0	Y
A-5-0-0	Z
C-5-0-0	Alpha
E-5-0-0	Bravo
0-6-0-0	Charlie
2-6-0-0	Delta
4-6-0-0	Echo
6-6-0-0	Foxtrot
8-6-0-0	Golf
A-6-0-0	Hotel
C-6-0-0	India
E-6-0-0	Juliet
0-7-0-0	Kilo
2-7-0-0	Lima
4-7-0-0	Mike
6-7-0-0	November
8-7-0-0	Oscar
A-7-0-0	Papa
C-7-0-0	Quebec
E-7-0-0	Romeo
0-8-0-0	Sierra
2-8-0-0	Tango
4-8-0-0	Uniform
6-8-0-0	Victor
8-8-0-0	Whiskey
A-8-0-0	X-Ray
C-8-0-0	Yankee
E-8-0-0	Zulu
0-9-0-0	And
2-9-0-0	The
4-9-0-0	Amps
6-9-0-0	Hertz
8-9-0-0	Farad
A-9-0-0	Watts
C-9-0-0	Mega
E-9-0-0	Micro
0-A-0-0	Milli
2-A-0-0	Meter

Code	Word
4-A-0-0	Pico
6-A-0-0	Ohms
8-A-0-0	Caution
A-A-0-0	Danger
C-A-0-0	Fire
E-A-0-0	Area
0-B-0-0	Light
2-B-0-0	Pressure
4-B-0-0	Power
6-B-0-0	Circuit
8-B-0-0	Check
A-B-0-0	Change
C-B-0-0	Complete
E-B-0-0	Connect
0-C-0-0	Degrees
2-C-0-0	Minus
4-C-0-0	Repair
6-C-0-0	Seconds
8-C-0-0	Service
A-C-0-0	Not
C-C-0-0	Temperature
E-C-0-0	Unit
0-D-0-0	Switch
2-D-0-0	Start
4-D-0-0	Stop
6-D-0-0	Timer
8-D-0-0	Valve
A-D-0-0	Line
C-D-0-0	Machine
E-D-0-0	Up
0-E-0-0	Down
2-E-0-0	Off
4-E-0-0	On
6-E-0-0	Is
8-E-0-0	Number
A-E-0-0	Time
C-E-0-0	Control
E-E-0-0	Alert
0-F-0-0	Out
2-F-0-0	Automatic
4-F-0-0	Electrician
6-F-0-0	Adjust
8-F-0-0	Point
A-F-0-0	Wait

Hex Address	Word
C-F-0-0	At
E-F-0-0	Between
0-0-1-0	Break
2-0-1-0	Smoke
4-0-1-0	Red
6-0-1-0	Minutes
8-0-1-0	Hours
A-0-1-0	Abort
C-0-1-0	All
E-0-1-0	Button
0-1-1-0	Calibrate
2-1-1-0	Call
4-1-1-0	Cancel
6-1-1-0	Clock
8-1-1-0	Crane
A-1-1-0	Cycle
C-1-1-0	Days
E-1-1-0	Device
0-2-1-0	Direction
2-2-1-0	Display
4-2-1-0	Door
6-2-1-0	East
8-2-1-0	Enter
A-2-1-0	Equal
C-2-1-0	Exit
E-2-1-0	Fail
0-3-1-0	Feet
2-3-1-0	Fast
4-3-1-0	Flow
6-3-1-0	Frequency
8-3-1-0	From
A-3-1-0	About
C-3-1-0	Gage
E-3-1-0	Gate
0-4-1-0	Get
2-4-1-0	Go
4-4-1-0	Green
6-4-1-0	High
8-4-1-0	Hold
A-4-1-0	Inch
C-4-1-0	Inspector
E-4-1-0	Intruder

0-5-1-0	Left
2-5-1-0	Low
4-5-1-0	Manual
6-5-1-0	Measure
8-5-1-0	Mill
A-5-1-0	Motor
C-5-1-0	Move
E-5-1-0	North
0-6-1-0	Of
2-6-1-0	Open
4-6-1-0	Over
6-6-1-0	Pass
8-6-1-0	Passed
A-6-1-0	Percent
C-6-1-0	Plus
E-6-1-0	Position
0-7-1-0	Press
2-7-1-0	Probe
4-7-1-0	Pull
6-7-1-0	Push
8-7-1-0	Range
A-7-1-0	Ready
C-7-1-0	Repeat
E-7-1-0	Right
0-8-1-0	Safe
2-8-1-0	Set
4-8-1-0	Shut
6-8-1-0	Slow
8-8-1-0	South
A-8-1-0	Speed
C-8-1-0	Test
E-8-1-0	Tool
0-9-1-0	Turn
2-9-1-0	Under
4-9-1-0	Volts
6-9-1-0	West
8-9-1-0	Yellow

LOAD ADDRESS, label the ROM location, identify the data, and tell the TMS5110A to speak.

APPLICATIONS FOR THE LPC SYNTHESIZER

There are two different approaches for applying this TMS5110A-based circuitry. The first application is a practical one. By connecting the proper control equipment to The LPC Synthesizer, a large number of "talking" tools and appliances could be constructed. Each of these vocal devices would be able to respond to the user with their usual analog or digital display, as well as in a highly intelligible voice. For example, phrases that state time, temperature, and measurements are all easily created from the VM61006A vocabulary. In practice, you would have a multimeter that would "tell" you that a resistor's value is "two-hundred-twenty-thousand-ohms."

The second application, once again, demonstrates the remarkable utility of speech synthesizers in education. By developing a well-structured "shell" program that could manage the arrangement of each ROM vocabulary element, the student would possess a complete speech laboratory on his or her desktop. Such a program would turn The LPC Synthesizer into a "speech construction set." In this manner, by using each of the VM61006A's vocabulary words as a basic building block, each pupil would be able to receive a self-paced introduction into sentence-level grammar and syntax. Furthermore, by following the design aspects used in this project, as new TMS5110A ROMs become available, the effective "dictionary" could be increased and the degree of instruction expanded.

ONE MORE STEP

The future for LPC speech synthesis is only just beginning with the TMS5110A. A new chip, the General Instrument SP1000, is not only capable of LPC speech synthesis, but it is also able to recognize human speech. Now, wait a minute. Can you fully grasp the implications from this technology? This IC is actually able to understand and respond, via the right software, to a spoken command input.

The General Instrument SP1000 is a NMOS LSI device with a $+5$ V operating voltage (see Fig. 8-4). An 8-bit, bidirectional data bus configures the chip as an intelligent peripheral with speech recognition and LPC speech synthesis capabilities. General Instrument is currently developing an allophonic based synthesis program. The use of this program will enable the SP1000 to create synthesized, allophone-based speech.

During speech recognition, the SP1000 requires only a small number of support components. A combined external 8-bit A/D converter with sample, hold, and high-pass filter generate most of the control circuitry. An additional automatic gain-control amplifier reduces the overall amplitude of the incoming spoken signal based on an SP1000-based automatic gain-control algorithm. Finally, the now standard low-pass filter and amplifier section processes the SP1000's audio output.

When the final speech recognition circuit has been built, two special software programs are needed for proper operation. The first program

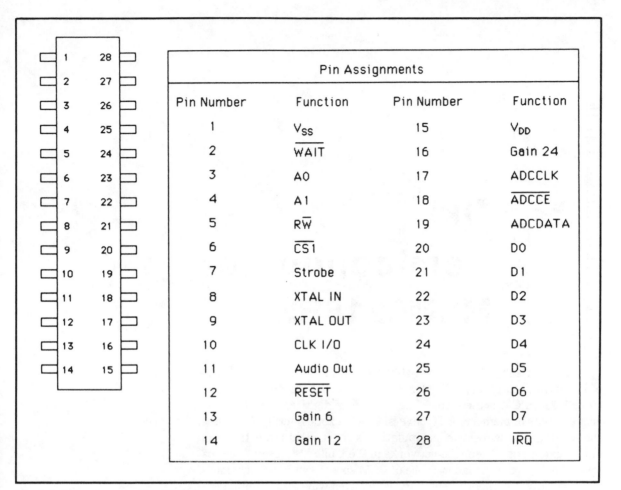

Pin Assignments			
Pin Number	Function	Pin Number	Function
1	V_{SS}	15	V_{DD}
2	$\overline{WAIT}$	16	Gain 24
3	A0	17	ADCCLK
4	A1	18	$\overline{ADCCE}$
5	$R\overline{W}$	19	ADCDATA
6	$\overline{CS1}$	20	D0
7	Strobe	21	D1
8	XTAL IN	22	D2
9	XTAL OUT	23	D3
10	CLK I/O	24	D4
11	Audio Out	25	D5
12	$\overline{RESET}$	26	D6
13	Gain 6	27	D7
14	Gain 12	28	$\overline{IRQ}$

Fig. 8-4. Pin assignments for SP1000.

"trains" the SP1000 to recognize your unique pronunciation traits and speech patterns. In order to ensure a properly trained circuit, the software should make several reads of each spoken command and create an average from these inputs. The second program is necessary in order to have your computer perform the action that you have assigned to each trained speech input. In fact, with the proper software control, you could finally tell your computer to take a flying leap. And it would.

9 Oki Semiconductor MSM5218RS

I**N THE QUEST FOR THE HIGHEST DEGREE OF INTELLIGIBILITY** in synthesized speech, Chapter 2 concludes that PCM or, more specifically, ADPCM is the victor. These forms of digitized speech rely on vast amounts of memory, A/D conversion, and exotic filtering. Of course, the result of this waveform manipulation is speech that rivals the original human input. Telephone networks in the United States of America, for example, make an elaborate use of PCM speech synthesis techniques.

Basically, the theory behind PCM involves waveform sampling after passing the input signal through an A/D converter. The changes in the amplitude are recorded as voltage levels over a variable sampling rate. Once the total input has been analyzed, it is stored in a memory device (e.g., RAM or disk media). Later, when this processed signal is synthesized, a variable sampling rate (identical to the initial rate) is applied to the voltage levels and changed into an analog signal by a D/A converter.

Enhancements to this basic PCM technique have been attempted and are annotated in Chapter 2. Most of these methods have met with various degrees of success. Usually the two prime obstacles have been the data bit rate and the amount of memory consumed by the analyzed speech signal. ADPCM is a successful solution to both of these hurdles. By using a special quantization formula, ADPCM has achieved both a low data bit rate and a reduced memory expenditure. In fact, it is only through

ADPCM that the intelligible qualities of digital speech can be brought to the low-cost speech synthesizer market.

THE OKI SEMICONDUCTOR MSM5218RS

The Oki Semiconductor MSM5218RS is a CMOS LSI package requiring a nominal power supply of +5 V (see Fig. 9-1). Serial PCM data is compressed to a selectable 3- or 4-bit parallel ADPCM sample. During the sampling process, a variable frequency of 4 kHz, 6 kHz, 8 kHz, or an external frequency source may be established by the user. If the external frequency mode is activated, a range of 0-16 kHz may be used. Two pins on the MSM5218RS control this sampling frequency (S1-pin 8, S2-pin 9). In order to obtain the 4 kHz, 6 kHz, and 8 kHz frequencies, a 384 kHz clock crystal must be connected between pins 22 and 23 of the MSM5218RS. You may use other crystal values, but the sampling frequencies will be different from these provided norms.

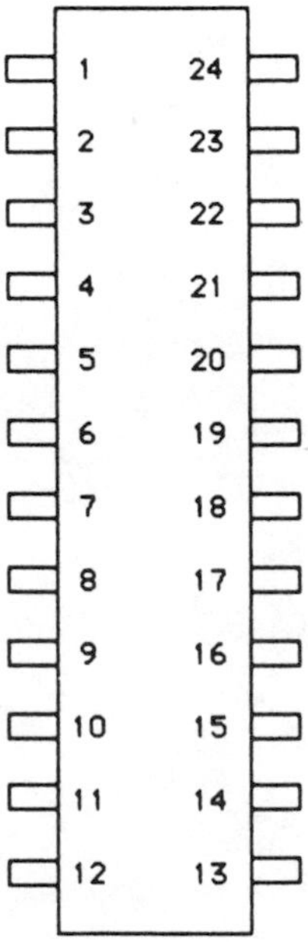

Pin Assignments			
Pin Number	Function	Pin Number	Function
1	V.CK	13	$\overline{\text{S.CON}}$
2	D0	14	SO.CK
3	D1	15	DAS
4	D2	16	T1
5	D3	17	T2
6	AN/$\overline{\text{SYN}}$	18	DA.OUT
7	4B/$\overline{\text{3B}}$	19	MSB/SO
8	S1	20	BIN/$\overline{\text{TOC}}$
9	S2	21	RESET
10	SI.CK	22	XT
11	ADSI	23	$\overline{\text{XT}}$
12	V_{SS}	24	V_{DD}

Fig. 9-1. Pin assignments for MSM5218RS.

Once the serial PCM data has been compressed to an ADPCM format and stored, it can then be synthesized through a reverse process. In this synthesis stage, the ADPCM data is converted to a synthesized PCM data code. Following a trip through an internal 10-bit D/A converter, the final speech is output in an analog form. Regulation of this complete analysis/synthesis procedure is provided through handshaking at the initial external A/D converter input.

In any ADPCM digital speech system, you will need to use low-pass filters at both the input and output. These filters are necessary to reduce extraneous signal contamination. On the input end of an ADPCM circuit, these filters are known as anti-aliasing filters. There are a wide variety of low-pass filters that can be used with the MSM5218RS. One such filter that is worthy of consideration is the MSM6912 switched capacitor filter that is manufactured by Oki Semiconductor. The most attractive element of the MSM6912 is that it contains both an input and an output low-pass filter in the same package. The input filter has an attenuation of 14 db at 4 kHz and a corner frequency of 3.5 kHz. The output filter shares a similar response curve.

All of this frequency manipulation is carried out "on-board" the MSM6912 through its switched capacitor filter technology. By using this technology, all of the frequency controls are performed without the need for supplementary frequency maintaining components. One precaution about the MSM6912 is the presence of a 200 Hz high-pass filter on the input filter line. This filter can be overridden by using the output filter stage of the MSM6912 as the input filter.

CONSTRUCTION OF THE ADPCM SYNTHESIZER

The construction techniques presented for this synthesizer are slightly different from those described for all of the previous projects. The reason for this approach has been to provide all of the basic information that will be necessary for building a complete ADPCM digital speech system. For one thing, this method allows for the painless addition of future technology to the circuit design. These factors include the rapidly changing field of high performance, dual function filters (e.g., the MSM6912). But don't misunderstand, this project is complete. All you will need to do is supply the current logic that correctly handles the required function.

Other than the clearly labeled user supplied components, seven ICs are used in The ADPCM Synthesizer (see Fig. 9-2 and Table 9-1). This large number of semiconductors will require a PC board with at least 36 sq. inches of surface area (e.g., Radio Shack #276-190). Contrary to the other speech synthesizer circuits described in this book, after you have soldered all of the IC sockets into place, only a handful of support components and some pin-to-pin wiring will be necessary for complet-

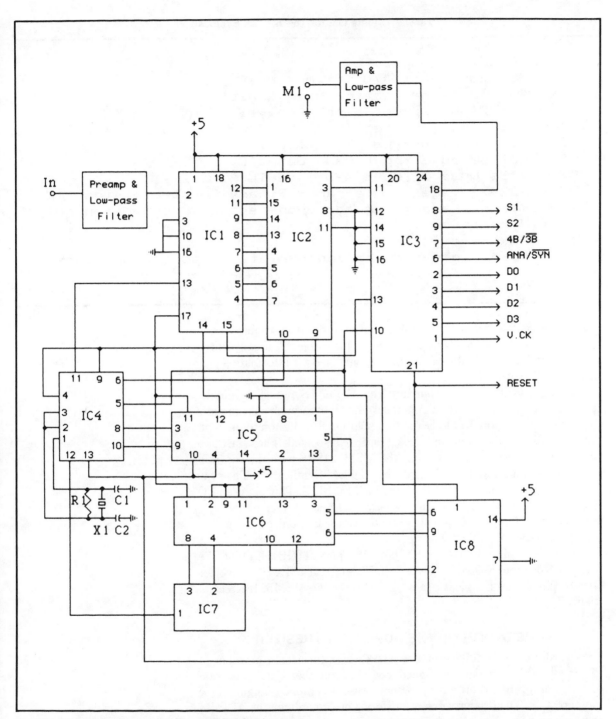

Fig. 9-2. Schematic diagram for The ADPCM Synthesizer.

Table 9-1. Parts List for The ADPCM Synthesizer.

```
C1, C2 - 220 pf capacitor
IC1 - MSM5204 8-bit A/D Converter IC
IC2 - 4014 8-stage Static Shift Register IC
IC3 - MSM5218RS ADPCM Speech Analysis/Synthesis IC
IC4 - 4069 Hex Inverter IC
IC5 - 4013 Dual D-type Flip-flop IC
IC6 - 4011 Quad 2-input NAND Gate IC
IC7 - 4081 Quad 2-input AND Gate IC
IC8 - 40247-stage Ripple-carry Binary Counter/Divider IC
M1 - external amplifier and 8-ohm speaker connection point
R1 - 1M resistor
X1 - 384 kHz crystal
Interface* - provide the appropriate support components
              for your desired interface
```

ing this project. A virtually digital design, like this one, requires little more than the ICs themselves. [Note: this digital project is ideally suited to a custom PC board fabrication. See Appendix B for information pertaining to this process.]

Your greatest concern in building The ADPCM Synthesizer is in determining an interface method. A parallel data input through a computer's expansion slot or port would be the best solution. In addition to the 8-bit data input line, a sync line and a reset line are also used. These last two lines would be used to synchronize the MSM5218RS with the controlling microcomputer and to initialize The ADPCM Synthesizer. The sync line is connected to pin 1 (V.CK) of the MSM5218RS. This pin is an I/O line that outputs at the frequency set by pins 8 and 9 (see above). By watching this line, the external computer can synchronize its input or output of data with this signal.

The reset line is connected between pin 21 (RESET) of the MSM5218RS and a Dual 'D'-Type Flip-Flop (4013) and a Hex Inverter (4069). When a high logic is received on this pin the MSM5218RS is initialized.

OPERATION OF THE ADPCM SYNTHESIZER

In order to make full use of The ADPCM Synthesizer, you will need to write two short programs. Speed is vital during the actual execution of these programs, therefore, you should use a compiled language for their creation. The first program is for storing or "recording" the ADPCM sampled speech. Basically, this program will first activate the ADPCM circuit. Then, by using the pulse on the sync line, this program will "read" each 4-bit data line address (D0-D3). After two reads, these two nibbles can be combined into a byte and stored in a memory buffer. You could make this program even more deluxe by providing a "save to disk" option. ADPCM speech data can quickly consume great quantities of memory, therefore, allow for an ample buffer size.

Now that you have a disk full of ADPCM-coded speech, you will need your second program to be able to listen to these digitized utterances. This "playback" program watches the sync line and inputs the ADPCM code into the MSM5218RS on each pulse. Prior to using this program, you must be sure to set pin 6 (ANA/SYN) of the MSM5218RS to a low logic. This turns the MSM5218RS into its synthesis mode and deactivates its analysis mode. An external amplifier and speaker arrangement will have to be used during this ADPCM playback. The digitized sounds that you will hear (you can use music, as well as speech with The ADPCM Synthesizer) are far superior to the allophonic vocalizations that were possible with the synthesizer in Chapter 3.

APPLICATIONS FOR THE ADPCM SYNTHESIZER

ADPCM's ability to encode any form of sound opens a huge application vista for The ADPCM Synthesizer. No longer are you saddled with a strictly speech-oriented synthesizer. You are now able, with the appropriate computer control, to record your own custom vocabulary for subsequent usage. The degree of flexibility offered by this ability is perfect for several household applications.

Anytime you need a specific "canned" phrase to be delivered in the most intelligible manner, ADPCM speech synthesis is the ticket. Granted, many of the applications that require this degree of comprehension would be better suited to magnetic storage on a conventional tape recording system. In situations that dictate the presence of a computer, however, the digitally saved ADPCM speech would be the best choice. The area of household control and security is a representative field that would benefit from this type of system. For example, each appliance could be assigned a specific phrase for either a secure or a violated nature. This spoken response is then given during each routine status report.

Of course, this type of application could be just as easily handled by any ROM-based LPC or formant speech synthesizer. Even the recording of digital music can be duplicated with comparable fidelity in an analog fashion. The real tip of the application iceberg is in recording these ADPCM digital waveforms for future use in a speech recognition system. By sending the analog speech signal to the computer in a digital form, over half the battle for this simple speech recognition system has been won. These ADPCM encoded words, phrases, and sentences, once they have been stored inside the computer, can be run through a battery of conditional clauses until a match is made. A successful match is then branched to an execution subroutine where the spoken word is turned into a computer action. For the handicapped person, this would mean complete computer control through the exclusive use of the voice.

ONE MORE STEP

There are two other Oki Semiconductor ADPCM IC's that offer interesting user options for digital speech. The MSM5205RS is a ADPCM synthesis-only CMOS device with a 3- or 4-bit ADPCM expansion synthesizer (see Fig. 9-3). Once the 12-bit PCM data has been reconstructed from the ADPCM encodings, a 10-bit D/A converter generates the final analog signal. Many of the same features of the MSM5218RS are found on this ADPCM synthesizer (e.g., 4 frequency sampling rates, external clock crystal, 3- or 4-bit ADPCM data, sync line, reset line). The major difference is that the MSM5205RS lacks the analysis stage found in the MSM5218RS. Two spin-offs from this deficiency are a lower chip cost and a reduced circuit population. Under normal conditions the MSM5205RS is used in designs that require only the synthesis of prerecorded ADPCM speech.

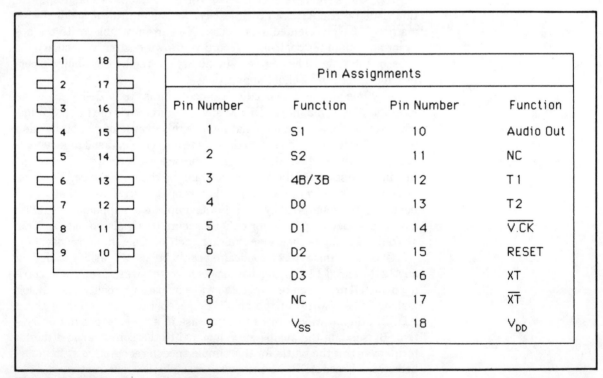

Pin Assignments			
Pin Number	Function	Pin Number	Function
1	S1	10	Audio Out
2	S2	11	NC
3	4B/3B	12	T1
4	D0	13	T2
5	D1	14	$\overline{\text{V.CK}}$
6	D2	15	RESET
7	D3	16	XT
8	NC	17	$\overline{\text{XT}}$
9	V_{SS}	18	V_{DD}

Fig. 9-3. Pin assignment for MSM5205RS.

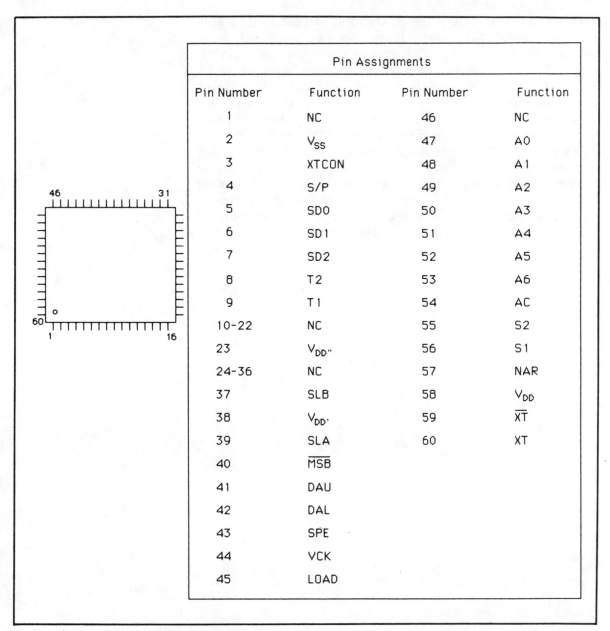

Pin Assignments			
Pin Number	Function	Pin Number	Function
1	NC	46	NC
2	V_{SS}	47	A0
3	XTCON	48	A1
4	S/P	49	A2
5	SD0	50	A3
6	SD1	51	A4
7	SD2	52	A5
8	T2	53	A6
9	T1	54	AC
10-22	NC	55	S2
23	V_{DD}"	56	S1
24-36	NC	57	NAR
37	SLB	58	V_{DD}
38	V_{DD}·	59	$\overline{XT}$
39	SLA	60	XT
40	$\overline{MSB}$		
41	DAU		
42	DAL		
43	SPE		
44	VCK		
45	LOAD		

Fig. 9-4. Pin assignment for MSM6202GSK.

The other Oki Semiconductor ADPCM chip is the MSM6202GSK. This ADPCM synthesis-only CMOS package adds an on-board 18K byte storage ROM to the features of the MSM5205RS (see Fig. 9-4). This storage ROM is a programmable area that can hold a maximum of 15 seconds of ADPCM encoded speech. Once this ADPCM code has been burned into the ROM, the user has 125 (three of the true 128 are reserved for the END phrase code [0000000] and two test codes [0111111, 1111111]) different possible entry points. The main advantage to this method of access is that the 15 second ROM-stored phrase can be broken down into separate words or, even, syllables through these various entry points. Therefore, with a little effort, an extremely intelligible phoneme synthesizer could be designed around the MSM6202GSK. But don't expect to see this development in the near future. Aside from the cost restrictions (a formant synthesizer is less expensive to produce than the a custom LSI ROM-based ADPCM synthesizer), the programming of the ROM is only licensed to Oki Semiconductor representatives and developers. In fact, polluting an ADPCM system with a phoneme ROM would be like making an omlet with a sledgehammer. They both suffer from the preparation.

Section III

Commercially Noteworthy Speech Synthesizers

N̲O MATTER WHICH BRAND OF PERSONAL MICROCOMPUTER YOU
own, there is a speech synthesizer for you. The current crop of commercial speech synthesizers, to a certain degree, lack the technological sophistication that is contained in many of the projects in Section I and II. For example, none of today's speech synthesizer products utilize the ADPCM speech synthesis method. Chapter 8 provides you with the complete instructions that are necessary for constructing an ADPCM system. There is one distinct advantage that the commercial speech synthesizer has over the projects that are presented in this book—the marketed variety is pre-assembled and guaranteed.

Actually, there has never been a better time to shop for speech synthesizers. The marketplace is literally bulging with hundreds of different vocal automaton manifestations. A realizable windfall from this market is that the buyer has the upper hand (which is a rarity these days) when selecting a suitable speech synthesizer. There are external speech synthesizers and internal, computer-specific speech synthesizer expansion boards. Additionally, there are complete microcomputer systems, as well as fully configured home robots that have speech synthesizers built into their circuitry. Finally, there is special software that brings the power of speech synthesis to a computer without resorting to supplemental hardware. This is today's speech synthesis market.

When there is such a preponderance of choices, there is a tendency for the buyer to become confused. Any form of confusion will completely negate the benefits of a swollen market. The solution is education. In this case, there is a need for a comparison of the features that constitute the difference between each of the market's offerings.

In this section, different types of commercial speech synthesizers will be examined: external, internal expansion boards, microcomputer systems, robots, and software. A Votrax PERSONAL SPEECH SYSTEM is the lone representative of the external speech synthesizer. There are, however, two members in the internal expansion board grouping—the MOCKINGBOARD B and the SLOT-BUSTER. The Commodore AMIGA is used to demonstrate a microcomputer system that has successfully melded speech synthesis into its design. On the other side of the coin is a robot with a voice—the HEROjr. Last, but not least, is a software package that brings speech to the Macintosh. This program is called SMOOTHTALKER.

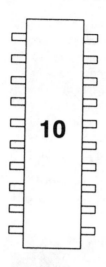

Votrax Personal Speech System

10

MAKING AN EXTERNAL SPEECH SYNTHESIZER CAN EARN A MANU-
facturer thousands of dollars of extra income. How is this possible, you ask? Simply because the potential user base is multiplied by the number of different computer systems that can utilize this external design. In other words, the manufacturer is not tied to a single computer system for the generation of sales possibilities. Essentially, it is this versatility that makes the Votrax Personal Speech System (PSS) so attractive.

The Votrax PSS is a "universal" text-to-speech synthesizer. All of the translation and speech duties are executed within the PSS. This "canned" software approach makes the PSS readily accessible to any computer user. Furthermore, the PSS is able to accept text strings from any computer system, exclusive of any special programming or transmission protocols. In simple terms, this means that the PSS is able to "understand" and speak any ASCII (American Standard Code for Information Interchange) text that is sent to it. The system is completely transparent to the manner in which the text is transmitted. This universality makes the PSS extremely attractive to a wide number of computer users.

FEATURES

In its appearance, the Votrax Personal Speech System is an odd bird.

Its domed, oblong, external shape doesn't conform to any of the configurations that are found in other computer peripherals (e.g., modems, disk drives, printer buffers) (see Fig. 10-1). Other than occupying more of your precious desktop space, this nonstandard external aspect doesn't present any application problems.

There are two control panels on the PSS—the front control panel and the rear control panel. The front control panel is sparsely appointed with a power indicator lamp and a volume knob. Moving around to the rear control panel is where all of the PSS's main connection and configuration ports are located. There are the expected On/Off switch and power connection port. Additionally, there are ports for attaching a Centronics parallel cable, an RS-232C serial cable, and an external speaker (the PSS does have a functioning internal speaker). The final port on the rear control panel is the DIP (Dual In-line Package) switch configuration port (see Fig. 10-2).

Three of these ports, the Centronics parallel port, the RS-232C serial port, and the DIP switch configuration port, are what provide the PSS

Fig. 10-1. Votrax Personal Speech System.

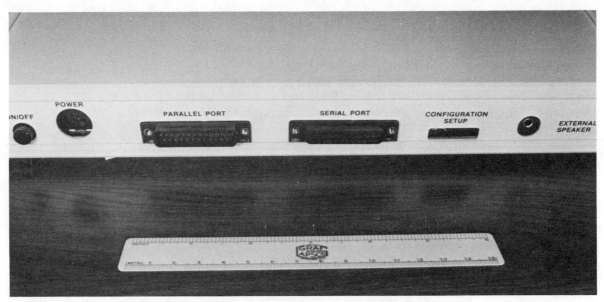

Fig. 10-2. Port assignments from left to right on the rear panel of the Votrax PSS: On/Off switch, power supply connector, parallel port, RS-232C serial port, DIP switch access port, and external speaker jack.

Table 10-1. DIP Switch Settings for the Votrax PSS.

Switch	Setting	Function
1-3	OFF-OFF-ON	9600 bps
	ON-OFF-OFF	4800 bps
	OFF-ON-OFF	2400 bps
	ON-ON-OFF	1200 bps
	OFF-OFF-ON	600 bps
	ON-OFF-ON	300 bps
	OFF-ON-ON	150 bps
	ON-ON-ON	75 bps
4	ON	XON/XOFF Protocol
	OFF	RTS Protocol
5	ON	8 bit word length
	OFF	7 bit word length
6	ON	Power-up message spoken
	OFF	Power-up message not spoken
7	ON	Parallel port active
	OFF	Serial port active
8	ON	Self-test mode
	OFF	Run mode

with its versatility (see Table 10-1). By providing the user with the option of using either of these popular ports for connection, virtually any microcomputer can be interfaced with the PSS. There is one caution when using either of these ports, however. Make sure that the pinout of the selected PSS port is compatible with the pin arrangement of your computer port. This advice is especially prudent with the PSS parallel port as it uses a DB-25 connector, instead of the more common Centronics type.

It shouldn't come as too much of a surprise to discover that the Votrax PSS is based on the Votrax SC-01 phoneme speech synthesis IC. Therefore, all of the standard SC-01 phonemes are available for implementation. Furthermore, speech velocity, amplitude, and inflection are all controllable with the PSS (see Table 10-2). The greatest benefit that the PSS has over a straight SC-01 is in its unique text-to-speech software. This ROM-based programming contains all of the speech rules that are needed to turn an ASCII text string into speech. Therefore, there is no need to learn any special phoneme coding sequences when using the PSS.

APPLICATION

Several types of data are recognizable by the Votrax PSS. These data are sent to the PSS in either an ASCII text format or as control codes. After processing these data, the PSS is able to utter speech, make music, and create sound effects. The easiest method for sending these data to the PSS is in BASIC through PRINT statements. Of course, these PRINT statements must direct their output to the selected port of the PSS. This procedure varies between computer systems; therefore, check your computer's manual prior to attempting this method.

The text-to-speech algorithm used in the PSS will be able to handle most of your daily vocabulary needs. Should the situation arise, however, where the PSS is unable to correctly pronounce a given word, you have two options. Your first option is to respell the stubborn word. This technique is called adjusted spelling. The purpose of adjusted spelling is to alter the true spelling of a word to a form that is more pronounceable for the PSS. For example, the PSS might not give you the desired pronounciation of the word "joking." By using adjusted spelling, you would receive a better pronounciation with "joe king." Granted, adjusted spelling does have the drawback of requiring unusual, if not bizarre, spellings. This complication can be avoided with the second option—user exception tables.

User exception tables compensate for deficiencies in the PSS text-to-speech algorithm by allowing the user to define the pronounciation of specific character sequences. Once this new sequence has been defined, everytime the PSS encounters this particular sequence of characters, the user supplied pronounciation will be used. This method is ideal

Table 10-2. Command Summary for the Votrax PSS.

```
Character                       Command

    @                           Attention
    @R                          Rate Control
    @(0-7)                      Inflection Control
    @A                          Amplitude Control
    @C                          Conversion Mode Control
    @V                          Voice Mode Control
    !                           Feature Control
    !(1,2,3)                    Musical Tone Control
    !A                          Alarm Control
    !B                          Baud Control
    !E                          Envelope Control
    !F                          Filter Control
    !L                          Load Control
    !N                          Noise Control
    !P                          Prompt Control
    !T                          Tempo Control
    !W                          Wait Control
  [ESC]                         Attention Control
  [ESC]C                        Connect I/O
  [ESC]M                        Mode Set
  [ESC]P                        Power-up
  [ESC]Q                        Quit
  [ESC]R                        Reserve Memory
  [ESC]S                        Special Characters
  [ESC]T                        Time Set
  [ESC]V                        Speak Version
```

for instances where a difficult proper name is frequently used (e.g., Prochnow) and when technical terms leave the PSS tongue tied (e.g., cnidarians).

The PSS can create user exception tables for either text sequences or phoneme sequences. Replacing text sequences is very similar to adjusted spelling. The only difference between these two methods is that adjusted spelling must be performed for every occurrence, while user exception tables need to be created only once. For example, when replacing a text sequence:

1) Determine a better, more pronounciable spelling for the text sequence. Prochnow = Prock no

Fig. 10-3. A special RS-232C cartridge is necessary for operating the Votrax PSS with a Commodore 64.

2) Load this new spelling into the exception table.
!LXPROCHNOW = TPROCK NO
3) Enable the exception table. @C1

A similar procedure is used for phoneme sequence replacement, except phonemes are substituted for the adjusted spelling.

PROGRAMMING

The following simple program demonstrates one of the possible applications for the Votrax Personal Speech System. This program is written for the Commodore 64 computer and the PSS (see Fig. 10-3).

```
10   OPEN 1,2,0,CHR$(6)
20   LET A$ = "HELLO, MY NAME IS PSS."
30   PRINT#1,A$
40   CLOSE 1
```

This program is designed for the Commodore 64's serial RS-232C port option.

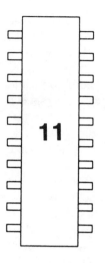

Mockingboard B

ADDING COMPUTER PERIPHERALS TO YOUR COMPUTER SYSTEM also adds an unexpected annoyance—the external power supply. These large, black, and heavy desktop wasters can turn a once sleek self-contained microcomputer into a power cord octopus. An even more subtle disaster can develop from running all of these power supplies from the same wall outlet. In addition to overtaxing the power capability of this single outlet, there is even the possibility of transmitting electromagnetic interference over the power lines and into your computer system. This interference can range from a slightly bothersome monitor static to the much more serious loss of data. Thankfully, some computer peripherals offer salvation from this external power supply dilemma. This deliverance comes in the form of internal computer expansion boards.

Internal computer expansion boards not only provide the computer user with a clean desktop, they also eliminate dependence on any external power supply. Microcomputers, like those of the IBM PC genre and the Apple *II*e, are equipped with special internal expansion slots. Each of these slots is supplied with its own power source. Therefore, peripherals, such as speech synthesizers, can be held invisibly inside the user's computer and activated on demand in the same manner as their external brethren. The leader in this field of internal speech synthesizers for Apple II family is Sweet Micro Systems, Inc. Their speech synthesis product, the Mockingboard B, is a unique chip/software package that mates with another Sweet Micro Systems product, the Mockingboard

A. The result is a powerful music, sound effects, and speech board with true stereo capability.

FEATURES

The Mockingboard B is nothing more than a speech synthesis IC (an SSI 263A), text-to-speech software, and a special game program. Please be assured that this description isn't intended to malign the superlative Mockingboard B. It's just a fact that the Mockingboard B is a peripheral's peripheral. In other words, the Mockingboard B is intended to fit into an empty socket (there are actually two sockets so that stereo speech may be used) on the Mockingboard A base unit. One advantage to this independent upgrade method is that you are able to configure your Mockingboard system to meet both your needs and your budget (e.g., some people might not want stereo speech).

Installing the Mockingboard B involves the plugging of the speech IC into one of the two empty 24-pin sockets on the Mockingboard A. After you have accomplished this task, just insert the Mockingboard C (when a Mockingboard B is added to a Mockingboard A, the result is a Mockingboard C) into slot #4 of your Apple *II*e. You are now ready to make your Apple speak. In order to make sure that you have correctly installed the Mockingboard B, Sweet Micro Systems has included an exciting demonstration program that lets you show off your vocal Apple. This demonstration disk also contains a text-to-speech algorithm. This text-to-speech algorithm can be accessed from a rule editor which provides a modest control over the conversion of words and phrases into Apple speech. Additionally, for those of you who are in a more playful mood, Sweet Micro Systems also provides an arcade-like game, "Battle Cruiser SMS 2000," that combines graphics with speech and sound effects.

If you are adventuresome, there is a cheaper way to get stereo sound with your Mockingboard B. Instead of purchasing two Mockingboard B packages (you will be paying for duplicate software), buy one Mockingboard B, an SSI 263A IC, and a high-quality 24-pin chip carrier. First, install the Mockingboard B as previously described. Next, insert the SSI 263A into the 24-pin chip carrier. You now have a fully functional Mockingboard B without the software. Finally, install your software-less Mockingboard B in the same manner, but in the other Mockingboard A socket, as you did the original Mockingboard B. If you did everything according to plan, you should be the proud owner of a stereo Mockingboard C. See Table 11-1 for a summary of the test mode commands that you can use.

APPLICATION

In addition to all of the obvious programming and application uses

Table 11-1. Command Summary for the Mockingboard C's Test Mode.

Character	Command
R	Speak Again
N	New Entry
^S	Save Word or Phrase
^Z	Return to Editor
^A	Set Amplitude
^I	Set Inflection
^F	Set Filter Frequency
^R	Set Speech Rate Level
^X	Help Menu
Space	Advance One Page

of the Mockingboard B, Sweet Micro Systems markets three exceptional software application packages for the Mockingboard B: Speech Development System, Foreign Language Rule Tables, and Developer's Toolkit.

The Speech Development System (SDS) expands on the elementary text-to-speech rule editor that is provided on the Mockingboard B demonstration disk (see Table 11-2). Complete phoneme control over the text-to-speech algorithm is provided with the SDS (see Table 11-3). Even though many of these phoneme parameters can become quite complex, a graphic display system within the SDS makes taming these parameters

Table 11-2. Command Summary for the Mockingboard C's Rule Editor.

Character	Command
D	Delete an Entry
E	Edit an Entry
I	Insert a New Rule
T	Test Mode
U	Update Main Rule Table
^L	Load Rule Table
^P	Print Character Table
^Q	Quit
^S	Save Rule Table to Disk
^X	Help Menu
^Z	Select New Character Table

Table 11-3. Command Summary for Sweet Micro Systems' Speech Development System.

```
Character          Command

Left Arrow         Move Phoneme to Left
Right Arrow        Move Phoneme to Right
Up Arrow           Raise Bar Graph
Down Arrow         Lower Bar Graph
   1-4             Phoneme Duration
    S              Speak
   ^A              Display Amplitude
   ^F              Display Filter Frequency
   ^I              Display Inflection
   ^R              Display Rate
   ^S              Save
   ^T              Display Rate of Articulation Transition
   ^V              Display Rate of Inflection Transition
   ^Z              Return to Entry Mode
```

a snap. By using simple SDS control commands, you can change a phoneme's duration, inflection, amplitude, velocity, filter frequency, and transition rate. This flexibility allows you to customize the vocabulary of the Mockingboard B.

If you want your Apple to speak to you in German, then a Foreign Language Rule Tables (FLRT)—equipped Mockingboard B will turn the trick. This humble software package contains three special language rule

Table 11-4. Utility Program Catalog for Sweet Micro Systems' Developer's Toolkit.

```
        Rule Editor
        Text-to-speech Algorithm
        AmperMock
        Mconfig
        Slotfinder
        Speechck
        Dtect
        Cout Intercept
        Input Intercept
        Apple IIc & IIe Drivers
        Bfile Loader
        Rule Table Converter
```

tables: British, French, and German. A main menu facilitates the loading of the desired rule table. Once the specified language's rule table has been loaded, the Sweet Micro Systems' text-to-speech algorithm may be employed with foreign text. A nice feature of the FLRT is that all of the tables may be accessed from either the main menu or through your own programming.

The final piece of supplemental application software from Sweet Micro Systems is the Developer's Toolkit. Basically, this disk contains 12 utilities that will make life easier while programming the Mockingboard C (remember, that's the A + B) (see Table 11-4). Many of the utilities are invisible to the user during their operation. For example, there is a Developer's Toolkit utility that will examine the Mockingboard to determine the presence of an SSI 263A speech chip (Speechck). This vital utility can be used as an error checker to prevent a speaking program from hanging up due to a missing speech chip. Similar utilities will scan the Apple's slots in search of the Mockingboard (Slotfinder) and then convert your "Tools" disk to recognize this slot (Mconfig).

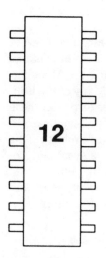

12

Slot-Buster

EXPANSION SLOT ADDITION SOMETIMES APPEARS TO BE EXPANSION board multiplication on the Apple *II*e. Your *II*e begins its life with a total of seven expansion slots. After you add a disk drive, an 80-column text monitor, and a mouse, you are left with only 4 slots for further peripheral expansion. Now, if you need a parallel printer port, an RS-232C port, extra memory (e.g., for AppleWorks), and a hard disk, you have just "maxed out" your once spacious Apple *II*e. Unfortunately, you have also eliminated your ability to add an internal speech synthesis expansion board. IBM PC owners have a solution to this slot ingestion nightmare—multifunction expansion boards. On the other hand, most Apple *II* peripheral manufacturers have blindly supplied their products as strictly solitary-function boards.

RC Systems is one Apple *II* peripheral manufacturer, however, that can save you up to four of your precious Apple *II*e slots. Their single expansion board, appropriately called the Slot-Buster, contains a parallel port, a serial port, a printer buffer, an amplifier, and a speech synthesizer. Each of these elements functions identically to their equivalent single-minded expansion board counterparts. Even more interesting, many of these elements can work together and produce a result that is unavailable elsewhere in the Apple *II*e marketplace. For example, you can "print" your ASCII text files through the speech synthesizer. This technique, when coupled with the on-board text-to-speech algorithm, will effectively read your memos, letters, and reports to you.

FEATURES

The features of the Slot-Buster are unheard of in an Apple *IIe* expansion board (see Fig. 12-1). There are two output ports—both a standard Centronics parallel port and a standard RS-232C serial port. One minor drawback to these ports is that they each require a special ribbon connection cable. These expensive "extras" represent the sole blemish on an otherwise fine product. Supporting these two output ports is a variable-sized printer buffer. This buffer can perform two distinct duties. First, it can act as a normal printer buffer and free the main Apple CPU from the drudgery of monitoring the printer. Second, and this feature is once again unique to the Slot-Buster, the printer buffer can act as a traffic cop and send the output to both the parallel and the serial ports, simultaneously. In effect, this technique enables two printers to print the same text, at the same time.

The two remaining features of the Slot-Buster deal with sound. Initially, the provision for an audio amplifier might sound rather extravagant. If you lack a special amplifier section on your monitor or if you find the standard sound output of the Apple *IIe* too "puny" for your tastes, then connect the two Slot-Buster amplifier cords and get ready to plug your ears. The resulting booms and zooms from your programs will turn you into a true proponent of amplified sound.

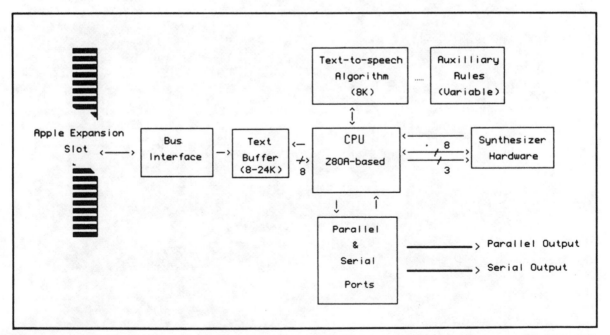

Fig. 12-1. Accessing the Slot-Buster's multiple features is controlled through an on-board microprocessor. (Redrawn with permission from RC Systems).

The other Slot-Buster sound feature is a speech synthesizer that is equipped with a text-to-speech algorithm. An SSI 263A IC is used to produce the vocal effect of the Slot-Buster (see Fig. 12-2). In an interview with Randy Carlstrom of RC Systems, the following reasons were cited for using the SSI 263A IC in the Slot-Buster:

We chose the SSI 263A for the Slot-Buster's synthesizer design for three primary reasons:

1. It offers unlimited vocabulary, using 256 built-in phonemes—ideal for a multilingual text-to-speech translation system as used in the Slot-Buster.

2. Requires a very low data input rate—typically only 200 bits per second (bps) for continuous speech.

3. Allows various speech attributes to be varied under program control, such as pitch and volume (necessary for generating inflection to keep the voice from sounding monotonic).

Fig. 12-2. A volume control for Slot-Buster's amplifier is located next to the SSI 263A IC.

Fig. 12-3. Slot-Buster is a full-sized expansion card that is best placed in expansion slot #1 of the Apple *IIe*.

APPLICATION

Even though the Slot-Buster is such a talented expansion board, let's concentrate our examination of its application ability strictly from the speech synthesizer viewpoint. Before any speech production is possible, the speech synthesizer port must be activated (see Fig. 12-3). This can be executed from either a hardware or a software approach. If you plan on using the speech synthesizer exclusively, then the hardware DIP switch settings should be used. Once you have gained the "attention" of the Slot-Buster's speech synthesizer, you have a choice of three different operation modes: text mode, character mode, and direct phoneme mode (see Table 12-1). Each of these modes presents speech in a different manner. When delivering commands to the Slot-Buster's speech synthesizer in any of these modes, you may use either absolute or relative parameters.

The first two modes send all received text through the text-to-speech algorithm. In the text mode, the text is read on a word-for-word basis. While in the character mode, the text is read on a character-for-character

Table 12-1. Command Summary for Operating the Slot-Buster's Speech Synthesizer.

Character	Command
PR#x	Activate Slot-Buster
PR#0	Deactivate Slot-Buster
A	Articulation
B	Punctuation Level
C	Character Mode
D	Direct Phoneme Mode
E	Enable Inflection
F	Formant Frequency
G	Glide
I	Enable Video
L	Load Auxilliary Rules
M	Disable Inflection
N	Disable Video
O	Change Port Assignment
P	Pitch
R	Clear Input Buffer
S	Rate
T	Text Mode
U	Enable Auxilliary Rules
V	Volume
Y	Timeout Delay
Z	Disable Commands
@	Reset

basis. The last mode, direct phoneme mode, however, circumvents the text-to-speech algorithm and permits direct user phoneme access.

No matter how comprehensive a text-to-speech algorithm is, some words are bound to be unpronounceable. To minimize these mistakes, the Slot-Buster has the ability to accept auxiliary rules. Production of these auxiliary rules is a complex task that is simplified through several utility programs that are contained on the Slot-Buster's utility disk. The standard format used in the production of auxiliary rules is:

$$L(F\$)R = P\$$$

where:

L- left context
R- right context

122

F$- text string
P$- phoneme string

In this case, the left and right context delimiters are used to define the exact presence of the text string. This format is useful when identifying a radically different syllabic pronunciation.

Another form of auxiliary rule definition can be used for specifying special character pronunciations:

$$(F\$) = P\$$$

where:
F$- character string
P$- phoneme string

This form is helpful when converting between English and foreign languages. For example, (1)=UH3 AH1 Y N S would speak the German word for the number one.

Amiga

AS SPEECH SYNTHESIS INCREASES IN ITS POPULARITY, MORE MAN-ufacturers are trying to incorporate this attractive feature into the design of their microcomputers. This vocal interest is in direct contrast to the major industry thrust towards graphics in the mid-1980's. Expansion boards, high resolution monitors, and custom LSI and VLSI graphics ICs dominated the list of essential computer criteria during this graphics push. Slowly, an emphasis is being placed on the sounds that a microcomputer is capable of producing. This aural excitement isn't being supported in lieu of graphics. It is really intended as more of a supplement to the high quality visual statement that is possible with today's super-microcomputers.

The standard-bearer of this new breed in microcomputers is a small MPU (microprocessor unit) manufactured by Motorola. While this chip is officially called the MC68000 16/32 microprocessor, it is commonly referred to as the 68000. Almost single-handedly, the 68000 has spawned a renewed consumer interest in the microcomputer industry. Technically, it isn't the public's interest in this new chip that has stimulated computer sales as much as it is the appeal of three new computers that are based on the 68000. The Apple Macintosh, the Atari 520ST, and the Commodore Amiga are the three top-selling microcomputers that use the 68000 architecture.

The presence of speech synthesis on two of these three computers, the Macintosh (see Chapter 15) and the Amiga (see Fig. 13-1), suggests

Fig. 13-1. A powerful text-to-speech algorithm is contained on the Commodore Amiga's Workbench disk.

that the 68000 is the first MPU with sufficient power to successfully con-
duct speech synthesis. A reexamination of Chapter 2 (at least I hope that
this is a reexamination) confirms the extensive employment of number
intensive operations in speech synthesis. In fact, the validity of this point

is further strengthened by the total absence of a conventional speech synthesis IC in either the Macintosh or the Amiga. Both of these computers use special software driven speech algorithms to produce their vocalizations.

FEATURES

Speech synthesis on the Amiga is directly accessed from Amiga BASIC. Through two simple statements, nine different voice parameters can be controlled (see Table 13-1). The actual control of these parameters, however, can be difficult to manage (see the following Amiga Programming notes). In order to avoid "Type Mismatch" errors, special programming steps have to be used. These precautions center around the requirement for integer arrays when specifying the control parameters. Even if you are unfamiliar with BASIC programming, the next section will have your Amiga "yakking" with a minimum of "hacking".

Only one of the two Amiga BASIC statements is used for manipulating these speech parameters—the SAY statement. Although playing around with these speech parameters can produce some exciting results, their use is not mandatory. There are system default settings that are used when the parameter integer array is missing. Another feature of the SAY statement is that it requires phonemes for its speech input. Luckily, this is not the case with the other Amiga speech statement—the TRANSLATE$ statement. The TRANSLATE$ statement uses a text-to-speech algorithm for reading normal English text passages. Combining the dual format SAY statement with the simple-to-use TRANSLATE$ statement makes the Amiga as powerful in speech output as it is in graphics production.

Table 13-1. Amiga BASIC's SAY Statement Array Parameters.

Array Position	Command
1	Pitch
2	Inflection
3	Rate
4	Voice
5	Tuning
6	Volume
7	Channel
8	Mode
9	Control

PROGRAMMING

Before you can begin BASIC speech programming on the Amiga, you will need both the Workbench disk (a copy of the Workbench is adequate) and a blank disk with *only* Amiga BASIC copied onto it. This two disk operation is necessitated by the manner in which the Amiga processes the BASIC SAY and TRANSLATE$ statements. The Workbench disk contains the speech and text-to-speech algorithms. Therefore, this disk must be in one of the Amiga's disk drives when a program using either SAY or TRANSLATE$ is run. If you have a one-drive Amiga system, you will be prompted when to insert the Workbench disk.

The other disk, the one that holds Amiga BASIC, is used to store your BASIC speech programs. This requirement might change with future releases of Amiga BASIC. Currently however, Amiga BASIC will only save BASIC programs on the disk that contains Amiga BASIC.

One final point to observe before you try the following Amiga speech programs, is to make sure that your system is properly connected to produce sound. Even though there are several methods to create an "audio Amiga," the best method involves the twin audio output phono jacks on the Amiga's rear panel. By using a phono jack Y-adapter, both of these outputs (left and right channel) can be tied together into a common output. This single output cable can then be connected to either an outside amplification/speaker system or plugged into your monitor's audio input phono plug (if your monitor has such a provision). A suitable phono jack Y-adapter cable that will work in this situation is made by Radio Shack (Catalog #42-2438).

When using the SAY statement, all spoken text must be converted into phonemes. The format for SAY is:

$$SAY\ T\$,I\%$$

where:

T$- phoneme text string
I%- integer parameter-array

The integer parameter-array is an optional expression and can be ignored. The following example will say the word "speak."

$$A\$ = "SPIYK"$$
$$SAY\ A\$$$

(Notice that Amiga BASIC doesn't require line numbers during program entry.) Now by adding a FOR/NEXT-READ loop, the nine parameters of speech can be placed into an integer parameter-array.

```
FOR P = 0 TO 8:READ I%(P):NEXT P
A$ = "SPIYK"
SAY A$,I%
DATA 220,1,200,1,20000,64,10,0,0
```

The other speech statement, TRANSLATE$, is more flexible in its usage. TRANSLATE$ accepts normal English text strings for input and converts this text into phonemes for the SAY statement. The format for using TRANSLATE$ is:

SAY TRANSLATE$ ("T$")

where:

T$- English text string

Therefore, in order to speak the phrase, "I like talking" with TRANSLATE$, you would enter:

SAY TRANSLATE$ ("I LIKE TALKING")

Actually, the use of TRANSLATE$ removes the chore of converting words into phonemes for SAY to speak. Unfortunately, words that are not in the Amiga's text-to-speech algorithm will have to be spelled with phonemes.

HEROjr

ENVISION THIS. YOU COME HOME FROM A DAY'S WORK AND OPEN your front door to a friendly, verbal greeting. Later that evening, when you leave to go to a movie, your departure is acknowledged and your home is secured from intruders. Finally, the next morning you are awakened by a singing voice that tells you both the date and the current time. What, you think that this sounds like a happy marriage to you? In this case, the proposal is electronic and not matrimonial. This is today's personal home robot.

Personal home robots made their first big commercial splash in the late 1970's. Before this time, robots served as expensive playthings with limited abilities. Then the robot "explosion" hit. A small cottage industry, resembling a similar development during the microcomputer industry's beginnings, of robot manufacturers was organized and a new market was born; or, was it? By and large, the personal home robot manufacturers failed to successfully address the issue of consumer interest. Then, as quickly as it developed, the personal home robot industry died down. Crawling out from this wreckage, however, is the lone survivor of the personal home robot market boom—the HEROjr.

The HEROjr robot is manufactured by Heath/Zenith. This 19″ tall robot has a distinguished heritage. Its parent, the HERO 1, served as the initial test bed for all of the features found in the HEROjr. This time-tested performance actually ensured the survival of the HEROjr over the rest of the, now extinct, personal home robot flock (see Fig. 14-1).

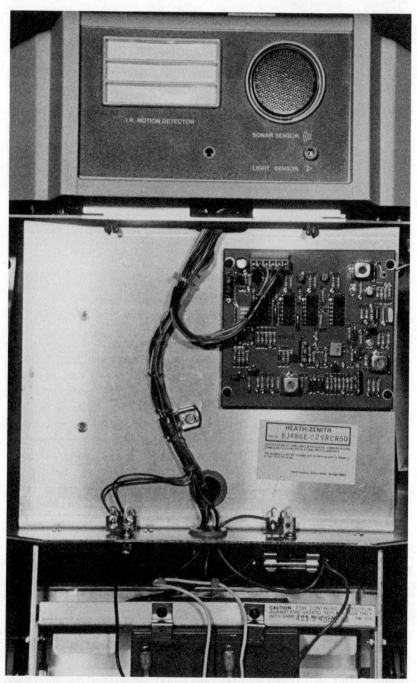

Fig. 14-1. Three of HEROjr's special sensors are visible in this "stripped" head-on view: IR motion detector, ultrasonic sonar sensor, and CdS light sensor. A plastic front and back panel hide HEROjr's internals during normal operation.

FEATURES

The HEROjr will be the first to tell you that it is your friend, companion, and home security guard. In fact, that previous sentence pretty much sums up the HEROjr's special features. Not only can it perform entertainment and security functions, but it can also talk and sing. The HEROjr uses a Votrax SC-01 phoneme speech synthesizer for these verbal interactions (see Fig. 14-2). This communication versatility is complemented by an extensive array of sensors. These sensors are used to navigate the HEROjr through its environment. Additionally, the sensors can be programmed to respond to detectable stimuli.

Using a human being as an analogy, the HEROjr is able to hear, see, move, and speak. All of these actions are under the control of the user without the need for a special programming language. An integral 17-key keypad, located on the "head" of the HEROjr, is used to enter control commands. These commands set the parameters used by the light sensor, ultrasonic sensor, sound sensor, battery-powered motor, and speech synthesizer. Hexadecimal programming is used primarily for this com-

Fig. 14-2. HEROjr's speech synthesizer, an SC-01, is IC U223 located in the lower left of the main circuit board.

mand capability. Remarkably, the user is completely unaware of the presence of this arcane hexadecimal notation. This "insulation" from hexadecimal notation is attributable to the speaking abilities of the HEROjr. You see, instead of displaying command entries on a monitor, the HEROjr speaks each entry, as well as providing the associated prompts, vocally (see Fig. 14-3). Therefore, the user follows simple English prompts with the required keypresses. Even though the majority of these key entries are in hexadecimal notation, the HEROjr applies comprehendible translations for each hex keypress. For example, when you wish to alter an entry, you enter a hex C. The HEROjr tells you that you should, "Press C to change." Now, that's what I call "user-friendly" programming. This interface is just one example of the excellent on-board software that was designed by Heath/Zenith programmers.

APPLICATION

There are two basic applications for the base model HEROjr: the

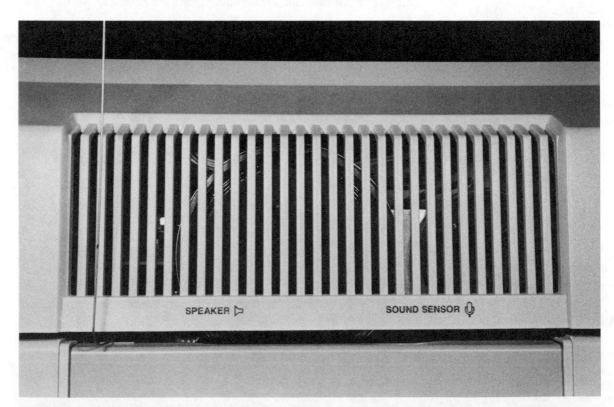

Fig. 14-3. An additional sensor, the sound sensor microphone, and the speech synthesizer's speaker are located on the side of HEROjr's head. The silver, vertical line to the left of the speaker is an antenna used for receiving radio signals from a remote hand control unit.

startup routine and the personality mode. While the startup routine isn't really an application per se, it is a vital element in the future programming of the HEROjr. The startup routine is performed only once. This is when the HEROjr is first switched on, after a prolonged period of non-Sleep mode charging. The Sleep mode is a passive charging condition which keeps all of the HEROjr's programmed functions in memory. Finally, the startup routine is an interactive application that requires user participation.

HEROjr STARTUP ROUTINE

During this explanation of the HEROjr startup routine, an arrow (>) will indicate the actions and speech of the HEROjr. User supplied responses will be indicated by an asterisk (*).

>VERSION 1.4
>CHECKING MEMORY
>TESTING BLOCK 0
>TESTING BLOCK 1
>TESTING BLOCK 2
>TESTING BLOCK 3
>8192 BYTES OF MEMORY
>CHECKING SONAR
>PLEASE WAVE YOUR HAND
  IN FRONT OF MY SONAR
*Wave your hand in front of the so-
  nar sensor
>SONAR-O.K.
>CHECKING STEERING
>STEERING-O.K.
>CHECKING LIGHT SENSOR
>PLEASE WAVE YOUR HAND
  IN FRONT OF MY LIGHT
  SENSOR
*Wave your hand in front of the light
  sensor
>LIGHT SENSOR-O.K.
>CHECKING DRIVE MOTOR
>DRIVE MOTOR-O.K.
>CHECKING SOUND SENSOR
>SOUND SENSOR-O.K.
>CHECKING MOTION DE-
  TECTOR
>PLEASE WAVE YOUR HAND
  IN FRONT OF MY MOTION

DETECTOR
*Wave your hand in front of the motion detector
>MOTION DETECTOR-O.K.
>SET CLOCK AND CALENDAR
>DAYLIGHT SAVINGS TIME SELECTED
>PRESS ENTER TO CONFIRM OR C TO CHANGE
*Press Enter
>ENTER
>DAY
*Enter number for day of week
>2
>ENTER DATE, MONTH
*Enter two digit number for month
>0
>4
>DATE
*Enter two digit number for date
>2
>8
>YEAR
*Enter two digit number for year
>8
>6
>ENTER TIME, HOURS
*Enter two digit number for hours (use 1-12)
>0
>2
>MINUTES
*Enter two digit number for minutes
>2
>1
>A FOR AM
>P FOR PM
*Press either A or P
>AM
>MONDAY, APRIL 28, 1986 2:21 AM
>PRESS ENTER TO CONFIRM OR C TO CHANGE
*Press Enter or C

```
>ENTER
>SET SPECIAL DATE
>ENTER DATE, MONTH
*Press Enter for no selection
>ENTER
>DON'T CARE
>DATE
*Press Enter for no selection
>ENTER
>DON'T CARE
>YEAR
*Press Enter for no selection
>ENTER
>DON'T CARE
>PRESS ENTER TO CONFIRM
  OR C TO CHANGE
*Press Enter or C
>ENTER
>I  AM  HERO  JUNIOR  YOUR
  PERSONAL  ROBOT.  I  AM
  YOUR FRIEND,
  COMPANION, AND SECURITY
  GUARD.
>READY
```

After you have completed the startup routine, the personality mode application is used to add some character to the HEROjr. There are six different traits that constitute the personality mode. Each of these traits is controlled through a select level value (0-9). Most of the traits have descriptive names that require little explanation: sing, speak, play, and explore. The two remaining personality traits, poet and gab, however, avoid obvious definitions. The poet trait speaks in nursery rhymes, while the gab trait spews forth random phonemes in a completely illogical fashion. By carefully determining the level values for each trait, the HEROjr's personality mode can be shaped in an almost human-like pattern.

PROGRAMMING

There are three different ways to program the HEROjr. The first method involves the built-in hexadecimal language of the HEROjr. An excellent example of using this native hex language is in programming both the HEROjr's name and the name that you want the HEROjr to use in addressing you. Access to this hex language is through a special keystroke (Enter + 0). You will know that you are in the programming

Table 14-1. The Phonemes and Their Hexadecimal Addresses of the HEROjr.

Code	Phoneme	Code	Phoneme
00	EH3	20	A
01	EH2	21	AY
02	EH1	22	Y1
03	PA0	23	UH3
04	DT	24	AH
05	A2	25	P
06	A1	26	O
07	ZH	27	I
08	AH2	28	U
09	I3	29	Y
0A	I2	2A	T
0B	I1	2B	R
0C	M	2C	E
0D	N	2D	W
0E	B	2E	AE
0F	V	2F	AE1
10	CH	30	AW2
11	SH	31	UH2
12	Z	32	UH1
13	AW1	33	UH
14	NG	34	O2
15	AH1	35	O1
16	OO1	36	IU
17	OO	37	U1
18	L	38	THV
19	K	39	TH
1A	J	3A	ER
1B	H	3B	EH
1C	G	3C	E1
1D	F	3D	AW
1E	D	3E	PA1
1F	S	3F	STOP

mode when the HEROjr states, "Robot Wizard," after you have completed the access keystroke.

Once in the Robot Wizard programming mode, you must enter the memory addresses that you will be changing followed by the new data. In the case of changing a name, this new data will be the hex equivalents for the desired phoneme string (see Table 14-1). Therefore, if the

HEROjr should address you as "chief," then the phoneme string would be:

T CH E1 Y F

This same string in hex would be:

2A 10 3C 29 1D

Finally, in order to tell the HEROjr that the data for the phoneme string is complete, the hex code 3E FF must follow the hex data string. This makes the final data code for "chief" as:

2A 10 3C 29 1D 3E FF

The second method for programming the HEROjr requires a supplementary ROM cartridge. The ROM-based HEROjr BASIC is a standard subset of the same BASIC language that is found in virtually every microcomputer. The major difference between this BASIC subset and the microcomputer variety is that you actually use your microcomputer as a terminal for entering your HEROjr BASIC program. Therefore, your

Table 14-2. Command Summary for HEROjr's HJPL.

Opcode	Command
0	Move
1	Turn
2	Sense Eye
3	Sense Ear
4	Sense Distance
5	Sense Motion
6	Sense Blocked Movement
7	Speak
8	GOTO
9	Key Input
A	IF
B	Compute
C	GOSUB
D	RETURN
E	Stop Motors
F	END

HEROjr must be equipped with an optional RS-232C port, before you will be able to program in HEROjr BASIC.

The third, and final, method for programming the HEROjr is with the powerful HEROjr Programming Language (HJPL). Whereas, HEROjr BASIC was a subset of standard BASIC, HJPL is a superset of the HEROjr built-in hexadecimal language. Like HEROjr BASIC, HJPL is contained on a ROM cartridge which plugs into the HEROjr's cartridge adapter slot. The advantages of HJPL over the lower hex language are found in the extensive use of op codes, operands, and structured program line numbers (see Table 14-2). Each of these features makes a final HJPL program easier to understand than its standard hex program equivalent. Best of all, you don't need an RS-232C port to use HJPL. All of its programming is executed through the HEROjr's 17-key keypad. Heath/Zenith has even thoughtfully provided a new keyboard template as a HJPL programming aid.

SmoothTalker

THERE IS A DISTINCT ADVANTAGE TO BEING ABLE TO SYNTHESIZE speech through software. For one, all of the hardware interface headaches are eliminated. Second, the cost of the speech synthesis product is greatly reduced. Third, and probably most important, the programming "kernal" that performs the real speech synthesis can be sold to independent vendors and placed in other software products. Of course, by this same token, other programmers can unlock and exploit these same speech synthesis software secrets. In one way or another, all of these things have occurred during the life of SmoothTalker.

SmoothTalker is a software-based speech synthesis product for the Apple Macintosh manufactured by First Byte (see Fig. 15-1). As with all of the previously discussed speech synthesizers (except the HEROjr), SmoothTalker couples phoneme input with a text-to-speech algorithm. The phoneme input in SmoothTalker, however, is used primarily to modify words that are mispronounced by the text-to-speech algorithm. Phoneme input is also the basis for developing exception dictionaries.

FEATURES

Since all Macintosh software must follow established user interface guidelines, SmoothTalker utilizes the mouse for the lion's share of its data manipulation duty. In other words, any command action or file ac-

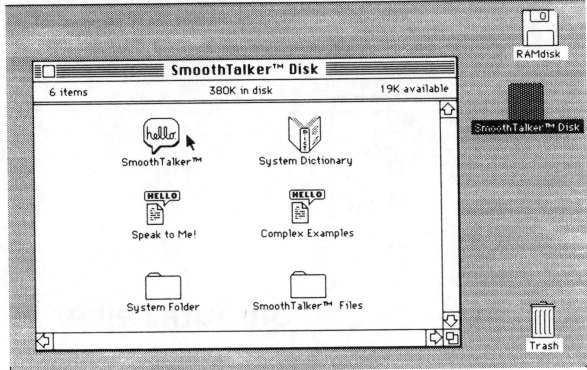

Fig. 15-1. SmoothTalker's disk catalog.

tivity is controlled with the mouse. The only other type of data input would be in either a text or phoneme format. But even these data need not be entered directly from the Macintosh keyboard. For example, previously saved Apple MacWrite or Microsoft Word documents can be read through SmoothTalker (see Fig. 15-2). It is even possible to use the SmoothTalker kernal within Macintosh programs that have been written with Microsoft BASIC.

There are five different parameters that can be altered in the SmoothTalker environment: volume, pitch, speed, tone, and gender. These parameters can be controlled either through embedded commands or through a special speech settings window. Embedded commands are marked by double arrows:

$$<<Vx>>$$

In the above example, this command would control the speech volume with a range from x = 0-9 (quiet to loud). Similarly, the other four parameters can be inserted into the text at any point.

If you wish to change the parameters for the entire document, a

Global Speech Settings Window will easily make all of the necessary changes (see Fig. 15-3). The Speech Settings Window is activated from the speech menu selection. This window contains a graphic display of the 5 speech parameters along with their current settings. Raise and lower buttons are "clicked" with the mouse to alter these parameter settings. Once you have established the desired parameter values, you must initiate SmoothTalker by choosing the Set Entire Document selection from the Speech Settings Window. This action will enforce all of the parameter changes throughout the entire document (see Fig. 15-4).

In an effort to provide the user with the most up-to-date documentation, First Byte does not supply SmoothTalker with a conventional instruction manual. Instead, the entire User's Guide is contained on the SmoothTalker disk. This practice allows the user to: print the entire manual, print portions of the manual, and leave a copy of the manual on the SmoothTalker disk for future "online" reference. The merit of having so many choices in preparing your documentation is overshadowed by having to use your own resources to produce the instruction manual.

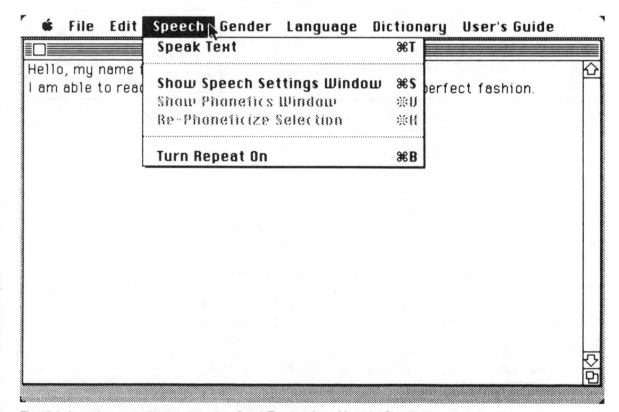

Fig. 15-2. Any written text will be spoken when Speak Text is selected from the Speech menu.

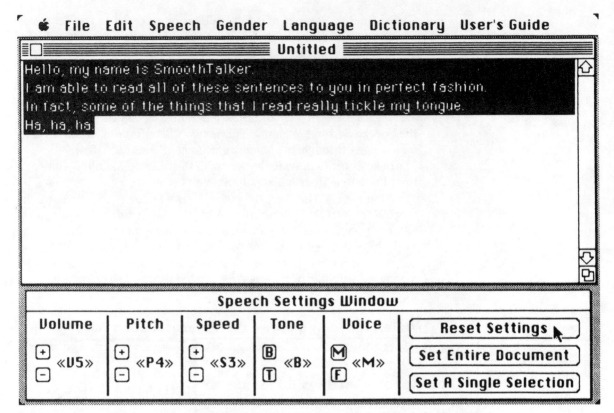

Fig. 15-3. Volume, pitch, speed, tone, and voice can all be altered through the Speech Settings Window.

APPLICATION

SmoothTalker applications are limited by their reliance on the SmoothTalker environment. This restriction necessitates the piping of all spoken text through SmoothTalker. If this isolation sounds like a limitation, you should switch to a hardware-based speech synthesis system. But in actual practice, the dependence on the SmoothTalker environment is irrelevant.

The ideal application for SmoothTalker is in reading your previously composed notes, memos, letters, and reports. Although this application sounds mundane and borders on being considered juvenile, you might find several hidden rewards in its adoption. Without a doubt, the greatest benefit will be in discovering syntax and typographical errors that your silent proofreading failed to uncover. In order to use this valuable editing technique, just open any MacWrite document (or Word document) that you wish to have SmoothTalker proofread. Next, set all of the parameters with the Speech Settings Window (don't forget to press the Set Entire Document button). Now, have SmoothTalker read your document to you by selecting the Speak Text entry on the Speech menu. When SmoothTalker has finished, return to MacWrite (or Word) to correct any faulty passages and to print your now "perfect" document.

PROGRAMMING

When programming speech with the SmoothTalker kernal in Microsoft BASIC, you must prepare your BASIC language disk prior to writing your programs. This preparation involves copying two files from the SmoothTalker disk onto your working copy of BASIC. Once these two files, FB Speech Lib and System File, have been copied onto the BASIC disk you will be able to write programs that can speak.

There is a new command that is available to you in this speech-enhanced BASIC—TALK. The format for TALK is:

$$\text{TALK } "T\$",G,L,T,P,S,V$$

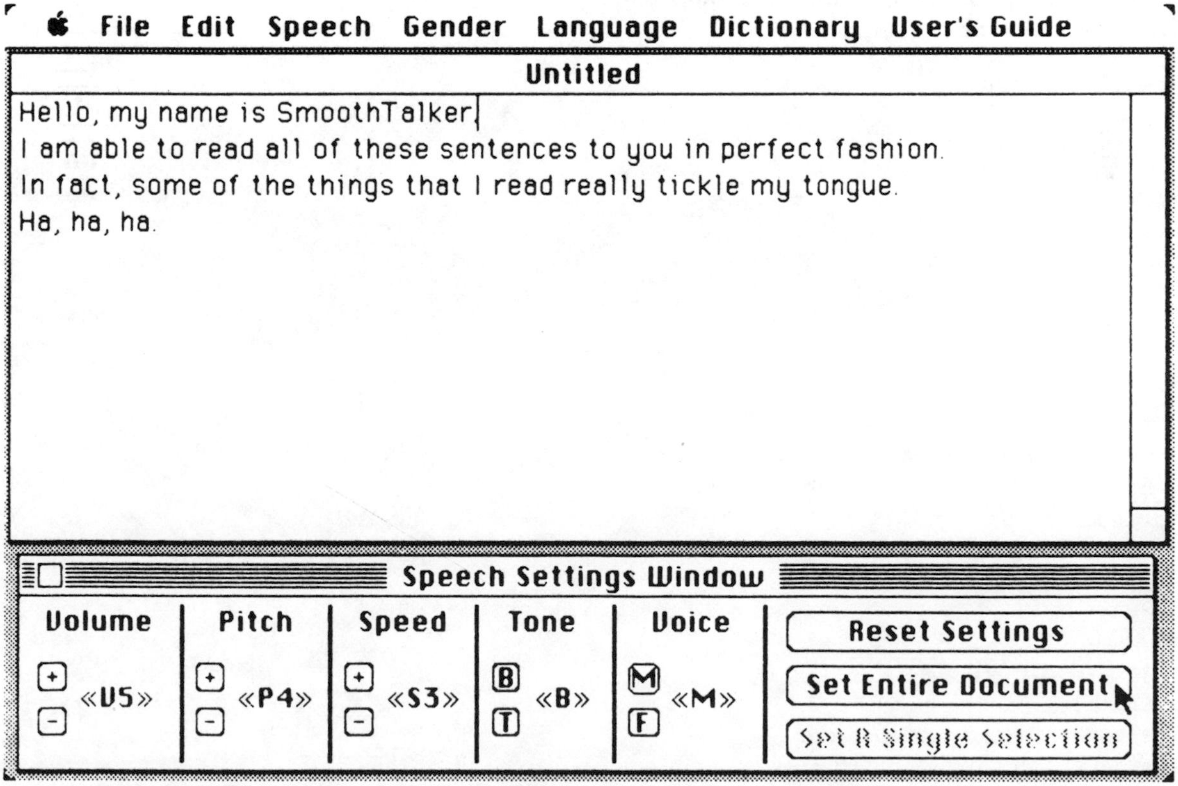

 File   Edit   Speech   Gender   Language   Dictionary   User's Guide

Untitled

Hello, my name is SmoothTalker|

I am able to read all of these sentences to you in perfect fashion.

In fact, some of the things that I read really tickle my tongue.

Ha, ha, ha.

Speech Settings Window

Volume	Pitch	Speed	Tone	Voice	
⊕ «V5» ⊖	⊕ «P4» ⊖	⊕ «S3» ⊖	Ⓑ «B» Ⓣ	Ⓜ «M» Ⓕ	**Reset Settings**
					Set Entire Document
					Set A Single Selection

Fig. 15-4. Text is highlighted as it is spoken by SmoothTalker. Words like "tongue" and "ha, ha, ha," however, are not in the standard text-to-speech dictionary. Subsequently, they are mispronounced with amusing results.

where:

T\$- a text string or phoneme string with a maximum of 250 characters
G- gender (0 = male, 1 = female)
L- language (0 = English)
T- tone (0 = bass, 1 = treble)
P- pitch (0-9)
S- speed (0-9)
V- volume (0-9)

You will also need to use the BASIC statement CLEAR (e.g., CLEAR,1024,1024) to reserve memory and the BASIC statement LIBRARY to define the speech library file (e.g., LIBRARY "FB SPEECH LIB"). Therefore, a BASIC program that would say, "I am SmoothTalker," is:

```
CLEAR,1024,1024
LIBRARY "FB SPEECH LIB"
TALK "I AM SMOOTHTALKER",0,0,0,7,3,6
LIBRARY CLOSE
```

Appendices

Appendix A

Speech Synthesizer Building Techniques

T HE LURE OF A TALKING CIRCUIT HAS A ROMANCE THAT IS ENJOYED
by few other electronics projects. By combining a few dollars worth
of parts with a speech synthesizer's schematic diagram, an instant "personality" is born. Unfortunately, several factors are bound to block the
successful implementation of digital speech. There are financial, mental, and physical reasons that might prevent the introduction of speech
into your computer's life. While I can't satisfy either your financial or
physical difficulties, I can try to help with electronics construction techniques.

Whether you are a seasoned electronic project builder, a casual computer user, or a budding speech pathologist who will be "firing up" his
or her first soldering iron, you will need to learn a few construction basics. Most of these building techniques center around the most effective
means to translate a speech synthesizer circuit from paper into a wired,
operating unit. Two specific areas in which this construction education
will be stressed are the manner in which the circuit is built and the enclosure in which it is placed.

Seasoned electronics project builders may be experienced hands at
soldering and printed circuit board (PCB) etching (if you aren't, see Appendix B), but the options of using the modular IC breadboard, universal PC boards, and E-Z Circuit boards are three methods of project wiring
are available to all levels of project builders. Speech synthesizer circuits
are easily transferred from the printed schematic onto a breadboard by

147

using easily cut jumper wires and no soldering. Circuit builders wishing more stability for their projects can quickly translate the breadboard circuits onto either a solderable universal PC board or an E-Z Circuit board. Radio Shack's MODULAR IC BREADBOARD SOCKETS (Radio Shack's #276-174 and #276-175) and EXPERIMENTER'S PC BOARDS (Radio Shack #276-170), Vector's PLUGBOARDS (Vector's #4609, #4610, and #4613), and Bishop Graphics' E-Z BUS BOARDS (Bishop Graphics' #EZ7472, #EZ7464, #EZ7402, and #EZ7475), are all well suited to speech synthesizer construction.

Once you have finalized your speech synthesizer design, it is time to place your circuit inside a housing. As a rule, a housing will only be necessary for stand-alone and parallel or serial port connection computer-based speech synthesizers. For example, if your final speech synthesizer project is for an internal expansion slot of an IBM PC, then you will not need to worry about a housing. Conversely, if your speech circuit uses a parallel port for interfacing with microcomputers, then you will need to consider the design of a circuit housing. In some ways, the familiar, boxy metal or plastic electronics project cabinet has turned into an antiquated relic. For the majority of the constructed speech synthesizers, however, the purchased storage cabinet is the ideal project housing solution.

PLUG 'N TALK

A great breakthrough in the electronics design community has been the introduction of the modular breadboard socket (see Fig. A-1). This tool will be totally alien to those of you who have never before designed an electronics project. But electronics enthusiasts have long employed these reusable boards to test circuits prior to committing the design to a final, soldered board. The reason behind this pretesting is really quite simple: why solder expensive components to a board, when the project's design might contain performance flaws?

The design of a modular breadboard is fairly straightforward: a hard plastic board provides a gridwork of connection slots into which the leads of electronics components are inserted. Electrical connection points are located underneath this surface grid. Without using any soldering, component leads are pinched in place by the underlying contacts. The connection slot spacing of IC compatible breadboards is situated so that integrated circuit chip pins fit neatly into the slots without being bent. Therefore, an additional benefit of the modular breadboard is its ability to accept ICs plugged directly into the board without an IC socket. If the builder then decides to alter a project's design, the ICs are easily extracted without damage.

Modular breadboard sockets are sold by a wide variety of manufacturers, but one particularly accessible type of breadboard is that sold by

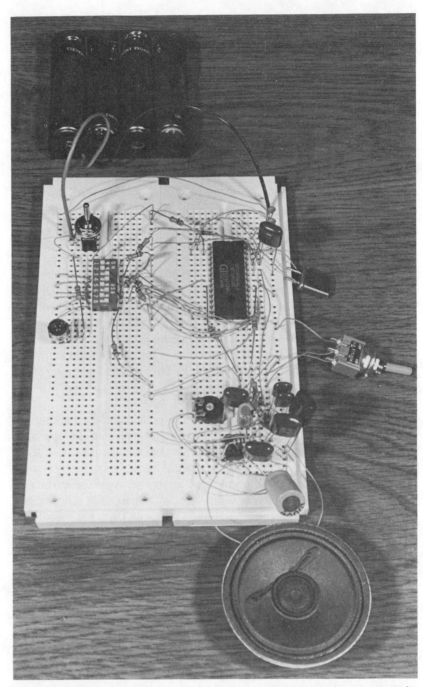

Fig. A-1. A modular breadboard socket holding a speech synthesizer project in its initial testing stage.

Radio Shack. This board comes in two sizes: the Modular IC Breadboard Socket (Radio Shack #276-174), measuring 2 inches by 6 inches, and the Modular IC Breadboard Socket (Radio Shack #276-175), which measures 2 1/8 inches by 3 5/8 inches. These two breadboards are designed so that they can be joined together in many different combinations and fit virtually any project size. The modular nature of these boards permits one to be linked to another through a tight fitting rim which runs around the edge of every board.

When a speech synthesizer circuit is constructed on a Modular IC Breadboard Socket, the underlying pattern of connection points must be remembered. The two strips of connection points, labeled X and Y, located along the left and right sides (in reference to the Radio Shack boards) each form a completely interconnected strip. These strips form a jumper bus along which component connections can be made. An ideal use for these strips is to designate one as the power bus and the other as the grounding bus. Therefore, any circuit connection requiring power can be slipped into the most convenient slot on the power bus strip.

Other connection points on each breadboard are united with their neighbors in strips of five horizontal connection points. These sets of connection points are numbered down the length of the breadboard. A separation running down the center of the breadboard creates a no connection "dead" zone between the five connection point strip on the right and the similar strip on the lefthand side of the board. This dead zone facilitates the placement of an IC onto the board across this gap without connecting the opposing pins of the IC.

Component leads are connected on the breadboard by making use of adjacent connection points; in other words, by placing the appropriate component leads next to each other on the breadboard (these leads can even be placed within the same slot). Alternatively, jumper wires can be used to connect one component to another over the surface of the board. Small pieces of wire wrap wire, with their ends stripped (approximately 1/4 inch of the insulation is removed from each end), are perfectly suited for such jumper applications.

The use of Modular IC Breadboard Sockets for initial circuit design preparation is ideal for the electronics neophyte. Even the more experienced project builder will find cause to use these breadboards. A speech synthesizer design can be tested, and, if the final results are not suitable, modifications are made to the flexible breadboard circuit. This technique reduces parts cost and saves the builder in final construction time. If, on the other hand, the builder decides that the speech synthesizer circuit is worthy of permanent implementation, the breadboard project can be translated in its exact form onto either a universal PC board or an E-Z circuit board by using the same component placement and the identical jumper wire locations.

UNIVERSAL PC BOARDS

When purchasing a universal PC board for your speech synthesizer's components four considerations are in order. First, a pre-drilled board is an absolute necessity; no one wants to drill dozens of holes to stick component leads into. Not just any pre-drilled PC board will do, however, because the chosen board must have IC spacing between its holes. This type of spacing permits IC sockets, or even an IC, to be soldered directly onto the board. Second, the board must have solder ringed, or pre-tinned holes. This feature simplifies the soldering process by helping the solder to stick to the board and to the component lead. Third, both sides of the universal PC board should be examined before purchase to ensure that the board does not have a specialized solder tracing pattern that will make transferring a breadboard design to the PC board difficult, if not impossible. Fourth and last, if the final speech synthesizer circuit is going to be connected to a microcomputer's internal expansion slot, then make sure that the PC board has an edge connector with the proper number of pads. A mistake at this point could jeopardize your Apple *II* project which needs a 50 pad edge connector.

Despite these four warnings, universal PC board selection is really quite simple. Speech synthesizer builders, using the Radio Shack Modular IC Breadboard Socket, will find the translation of their circuits to a hard-wired, soldered state easier than expected, thanks to two manufacturer's products: Radio Shack's Experimenter's PC Board (Radio Shack #276-170) and Vector's Plugboards (Vector #4609, #4610, and #4613).

The Experimenter's PC Board is specifically designed to imitate the function and connection points of Radio Shack's Modular IC Breadboard Socket. This means that specialized tracings do appear on one side of the Experimenter's PC Board. But these tracings correspond to the same vertical and horizontal connection strips that are found on the Modular IC Breadboard Socket. Because of this direct emulation, a breadboarded circuit can be exactly copied, component for component, jumper wire for jumper wire, onto the Experimenter's PC Board.

Because some computer-based speech synthesizers must be interfaced with a computer via its internal expansion slot, direct circuit translation with the Experimenter's PC Board is not practical. In these cases, the Vector Plugboards should be used (see Fig. A-2). Three types of computer expansion slots are represented by Vector Plugboards: Apple *II* family (Vector #4609), IBM PC family (Vector #4613), and Standard Bus (Vector #4610). Each of these boards is made from high-quality glass epoxy with gold-plated edge connector pads. There is also a helpful tracing arrangement that won't pose too difficult of a conversion chore when translating your design from a breadboard onto one of these plugboards.

Because some speech synthesizer circuits are not large enough to occupy an entire Modular IC Breadboard Socket, they can be planned

Fig. A-2. Vector plugboard #4609 is an Apple *IIe* bus compatible expansion card.

on the smaller Radio Shack version (Radio Shack #276-175). In this situation, it would not be practical to use an entire Experimenter's PC Board or Vector Plugboard. It is far more economical to cut one of these boards (either the Experimenter's PC Board or the Vector Plugboard) into two pieces and use the halved pieces to construct two separate speech synthesizer circuits. A small handsaw, such as X-Acto's RAZOR SAW BLADE (X-Acto's #234), is the perfect tool for this purpose. A careful cutting job, followed by a light sanding of the board's rough edges, will result in two ready-to-use miniature universal PC boards.

IF IT'S E-Z, IT MUST BE EASY

Custom circuit boards used to be the exclusive domain of the acid etched PCB. Now Bishop Graphics has introduced a revolutionary concept that could become the next dominate circuit board construction technique. E-Z Circuit, that's what Bishop Graphics calls it, takes a standard, pre-drilled universal PC board and lets the builder determine all of the tracing and pad placements. A special adhesive copper tape is the secret to this easy miracle in PCB fabrication.

The E-Z Circuit system is an extensive set of these special copper tape patterns and several blank universal PC boards. The blank boards

152

serve as the mounting medium for receiving the copper patterns. There are general purpose blank boards (Bishop Graphics' #EZ7402 and # EZ7475) and Apple *II* family blank PC boards (Bishop Graphics' # EZ7464). Each of these boards is made from a high-quality glass epoxy and pre-drilled with IC spaced holes. There is also a blank edge connector region on each board for attaching one of E-Z Circuit's copper edge connector strips.

Complementing the blank boards is a complete set of copper patterns. Each pattern is supplied with a special adhesive that permits minor repositioning, but holds firmly once its position is determined. This adhesive also has heat resistant properties that enable direct soldering contact with the pattern. An extensive selection of patterns and sizes makes an E-Z Circuit design worthy of consideration for speech synthesizer project construction. E-Z Circuit has available edge connector, IC package, terminal, test point strip, tracing, donut pad, elbow, TO-5, power and ground strip, and power transistor patterns. Additionally, each of these patterns is available in several sizes, shapes, and diameters.

Only four simple steps are needed in the construction of an E-Z Circuit speech synthesizer project. In step one, you will determine which pattern you need and prepare it for positioning. Step two is to place the selected pattern on the blank PC board. This is a simple process which involves the removal of a flexible release layer from the back of the copper-clad pattern. Step three is inserting all of the components into their respective holes. Finally, in step four, you solder the component's leads to the copper pattern. This step is just like soldering a conventional copper pad or tracing. If you use a reasonable soldering iron temperature, anywhere from 400 to 600 degrees Fahrenheit, you won't need to worry about destroying the adhesive layer and ruining the copper pattern.

Be sure to use an iron with a rating of 15-25 watts. Soldering irons that are matched to the demands of working with E-Z Circuit include: ISOTIP 7800, 7700 (the specifications for these two irons "press" the stated E-Z Circuit requirements, but they will work), and 7240, UNGAR SYSTEM 9000, and WELLER EC2000.

The result of this four step process is a completed speech synthesizer circuit in less time than a comparably prepared acid etched PCB. Incidentally, the cost of preparing one speech synthesizer circuit with E-Z Circuit versus the etched route is far less. Of course, this cost difference is skewed in the other direction when you need to make more than one PCB. This is because E-Z Circuit is geared for one-shot production and not assembly line production. Before you decide on your circuit board construction technique (Experimenter's PC Board, Vector Plugboards, or E-Z Circuit), read Appendix B for the latest advances in acid etched PCB design. Then evaluate your needs and resources and get to work on your speech synthesizer.

TAMING THE SOLDER RIVER

Before the first bit of solder is liquefied on your PC board, a plan must be made to fit the completed speech synthesizer project into an enclosure. Small enclosures are usually preferred over the larger and bulkier cabinets simply because of their low profile and discreet appearance. Space is limited within the narrow confines of such an enclosure, however.

It's quite easy to envision a two-dimensional speech synthesizer schematic diagram and then forget that the finished, hard-wired circuit will actually occupy three dimensions. Capacitors, resistors, and ICs all give a considerable amount of depth to a finished project PC board. Fortunately, the effects of these tall components can be minimized through careful assembly techniques (see Fig. A-3).

It is strongly recommended to leave all component leads at their full length while they remain on a breadboard. These ungainly components, however, do not permit the smooth translation of a project into a narrow enclosure, if they are soldered to the PC board in this same manner. With

Fig. A-3. Soldering speech synthesizer components onto a PC board can result in a nightmare of tangled wires and crowded components.

Fig. B-3. Quik Circuit's Mini-Finder menu. Layout is for PCB design, while Quote, Pen, and Print are used for making hardcopies of the completed design.

only a few exceptions, all components must be soldered to a PC board as closely as possible. One exception to this rule is in leaving adequate jumper wire lengths for external enclosure mounted components, such as switches and speakers.

Both component selection and their mounting methods directly affect a speech synthesizer's PC board depth. For example, the selection of a horizontally-oriented, miniature PC mountable potentiometer over a standard vertically oriented potentiometer may save up to 1/2 inch off of a board's final height (see Fig. A-4). Likewise, flat, rectangular metal film capacitors offer a space savings whenever capacitors of their value are required (usually .01 mF to 1.0 mF).

If a disc or monolithic capacitor is used on a circuit board, the lead can be bent so that the capacitor lies nearly flat against the PC board. The capacitor can be pre-fitted before soldering it into place and the required bends can be made with a pair of needle-nosed pliers. Be sure that the leads of every component are slipped through the PC board's holes as far as possible before soldering them into place. Excessive leads can be clipped from the back side of the board *after* the solder connection has been made. At this point a precautionary note pertaining to overly zealous board compacting is necessary. Do not condense a board's components so tightly that undesired leads might touch; a short circuit is the inevitable and unwanted result for this carelessness. Also, some components emit heat during operation. Therefore, some component spacing is mandatory for proper ventilation.

One way to minimize PC board component crowding is by using a special mounting technique with resistors and diodes. The common practice for mounting resistors and diodes is to lay them flat against the PC board. This technique is impractical, and occasionally impossible, on the previously described PC boards. A superior technique is to stand the resistor or diode on its end and fold one lead down until it is parallel with the other lead. The component leads can then be placed in adjacent holes..

One final low profile component that is an absolute necessity on any PC board that uses ICs is the IC socket. An IC socket is soldered to the PC board to hold an IC. Therefore, the IC is free to be inserted into or extracted from the socket at any time. Acting as a safety measure, the IC socket prevents any damage that might be caused to a chip by a excessively hot soldering iron, if the IC were soldered directly to the PC board. IC chips are extremely delicate and both heat and static electricity will damage them. After the speech synthesizer project board has been completely soldered, the ICs are finally added.

THE FINISHING TOUCH

The most easily acquired enclosure for your finished speech synthesizer is a metal or plastic cabinet which can be purchased from your local electronics store. Radio Shack makes a stylish, wedge-shaped enclosure (Radio Shack #270-282) and two-tone cabinets (Radio Shack #270-272 and #270-274), all three of which are perfect for holding your speech synthesizer. Another slightly less attractive, but still useful, project enclosure that is also available from Radio Shack is the EXPERIMENTER BOX (Radio Shack #270-230 through #270-233 and #270-627). The Experimenter Box comes in five different sizes for holding any size of speech synthesizer.

If none of these enclosures fit your requirements, you can also build your own speech synthesizer cabinet. The best material for building your own enclosure is one of the numerous, inexpensive type of sheet plastics that are currently available. Material, such as PLEXIGLAS, is easy to manipulate with the right tools and adhesives. Plexiglas sheeting can be cut with a hand saw or a power jig saw. Just remember not to remove the protective paper covering from the Plexiglas while cutting it. This will prevent the sheet from splitting or becoming scratched.

Construct all sides of the enclosure by adjoining sides together and laying a thin bead of a liquid adhesive along the joint. A powerful cyanoacrylate adhesive, such as Satellite City's SUPER "T" will bond two pieces of Plexiglas together immediately. Be sure that all panel edges are perfectly aligned before applying the adhesive. One side of the final enclosure design should not be joined with the adhesive. This panel will be held on with screws so that it is easily removed for future access to your speech synthesizer.

Hopefully, you have finished reading this appendix before you have started your speech synthesizer project's actual construction. If so, good; you have saved yourself several hours of headaches and, quite probably, several dollars in wasted expenses. If not, all is not lost. Just review your current construction in light of what you have learned in this appendix and make any needed changes in your construction procedures. At least, when you make your next speech synthesizer, you will know all of the secrets to successful speech synthesizer sustentation.

Appendix B

PCB Design
with CAD Software

F OR THE MOST PART, IF YOU OWN EITHER AN APPLE MACINTOSH
or an IBM PC family microcomputer, then you have the potential
for designing your own printed circuit boards (PCBs). This potential is
only realized after the purchase of some specialized design software, however. A rather general term is applied to this type of software—Computer-
aided design (CAD) software. CAD is a relatively young field with true
dominance already present in the IBM PC arena. This definitive CAD
software product is called AutoCAD 2 and it is manufactured by Autodesk, Inc. Don't be fooled by other CAD products that are designed for
IBM PCs and their clones and cost less than AutoCAD's roughly $2000
price tag. These cheaper programs are totally inferior to AutoCAD. Without question, the AutoCAD environment is the most powerful CAD software that is currently available for microcomputers and yet it remains
flexible to every users' demand. All of this means, that, if you own an
IBM PC (or equivalent) and need to design PCBs, then buy AutoCAD.
You will never regret your investment.

But what are PCBs anyway? PCBs are vital for the mass production
of circuit designs. The printed circuit board serves as the substratum
for building an electronics circuit (like a speech synthesizer). The board
itself is usually constructed from glass epoxy with a coating of copper
on one or both of its sides. By using a powerful acid etchant like anhy-
drous ferric chloride, all of the copper that isn't protected by a resist (a
substance that isn't effected by the action of the acid) is eaten away and

removed from the PCB. This process leaves behind a copper tracing and/or pad where there should be an electrical connection. The leading method for placing the areas of resist on a PCB is with a photographic negative technique. Basically, this technique acts exactly like its paper-based photographic cousin. In other words, parts of the PCB that are protected by the black portions of the negative are covered with a resist, while those regions that are exposed to the clear portions of the negative are removed by the acid.

Now that you know how a PCB is made, your next step is learning how to make a PCB negative. Until recently, your only CAD route was with the previously described AutoCAD. The cost in the IBM hardware alone was prohibitive to many designers. Most of this need for costly hardware changed with the introduction of the Macintosh. This graphics-based computer seemed ideally suited to the tasks of CAD. Apparently, two different manufacturers shared this same opinion and they each have created a breakthrough product for PCB design. QUIK CIRCUIT by Bishop Graphics (see Fig. B-1) and McCad P.C.B. from VAMP, Inc. (see

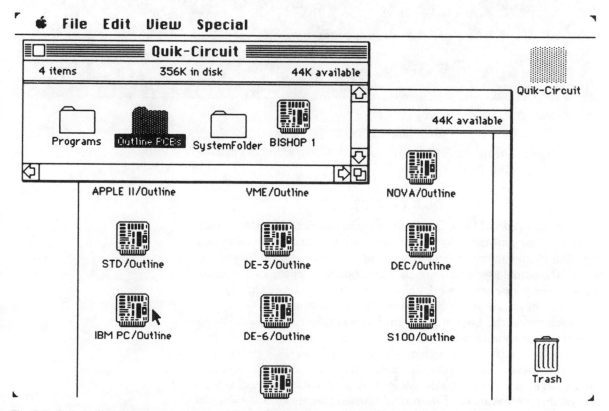

Fig. B-1. Quik Circuit disk catalog. There are a total of 10 different PCB templates for immediate use.

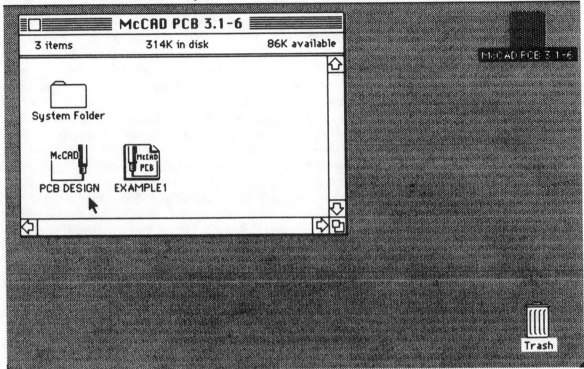

Fig. B-2. McCAD P.C.B. disk catalog.

Fig. B-2) are full-featured CAD programs that utilize a graphics environment for preparing PCB layouts.

QUIK CIRCUIT

The operation of Quik Circuit follows the standard Macintosh user interface. You start the program with a system boot and proceed through the Mini-Finder menu to the Layout program (see Fig. B-3). Along the way to the actual Layout program a dialog box will appear and requests the name of your current work file. At this point you may either specify a file that in progress or start an entirely new layout.

Once inside the Layout program, you will notice that Quik Circuit does use an elaborate menu bar. There are eight menus which contain all of the tools, scaling and patterns that are needed for PCB design. Additionally, there are two work area instruments—the Edit indicator and the Locator box. The Edit indicator is used for providing a visual indication of the current mode. For example, when you are in edit mode an "X" will fill the Edit indicator. Otherwise, an empty Edit indicator signals that you are in the active mode. The other work area instrument, the Locator box, displays the current coordinates of the cursor.

The procedure for creating a PCB with Quik Circuit begins with the setting of the grid size and magnification. You may now select your pattern from the Patterns menu. There are five unique Pattern menu selections. Each one, however, can be modified for any design need. These customized patterns are then saved with the Group and Store selection on the Edit menu. This modification function is a large bonus in Quik Circuit's favor. In practice, you could create a file that holds up to 21 different pin-size IC pad patterns. Then when your PCB needs an IC pattern, you can just access this custom file for the needed pattern.

One excellent beginner's feature is the online Help menu. This menu offers five different selections of help while you are in the layout environment. Each selection has a short summary of the major points that are important to its topic. For example, the grid size, view size, and zooming feature are all discussed under the Scale & Size selection. Even though you will quickly outgrow this assistance feature, it is a definite plus in

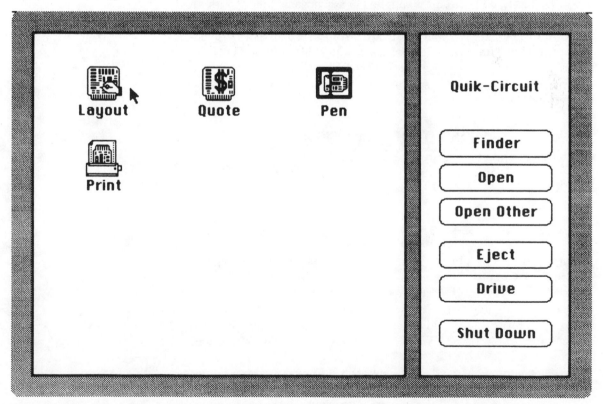

Fig. B-3. Quik Circuit's Mini-Finder menu. Layout is for PCB design, while Quote, Pen, and Print are used for making hardcopies of the completed design.

your initial PCB design stages.

When you are finished with your PCB layout, it is time to save and print your work. The Close & Put Away selection saves your PCB onto the specified disk and returns you to the Mini-Finder. At this point, you are able to make a printout of your PCB design. If you have an Apple IMAGEWRITER printer connected to your Macintosh, select the Print icon. If, on the other hand, you have a plotter attached to your computer, double click on the Pen icon. After the dialog box prompts you for the file to print or plot, you must pull down the File menu on the main screen.

Select the menu choice that is appropriate for your printer or plotter and begin the printout setup procedure. This procedure establishes the parameters that will be used during the subsequent printing (or plotting). For the best results, you should use a high magnification during the printing. This large printout will then have to be photo-reduced to the required dimensions of the final PCB. This technique ensures the highest possible quality in the PCB negative.

The Quik Circuit package itself is an anomaly in Macintosh software products. First, Quik Circuit is supplied in a handsome binder with an accompanying slipcase. Conversely, almost all other Macintosh documentation is wirebound with thin cardboard covers. Second, and most important, Bishop Graphics ships two disks with Quik Circuit. This little bit of insurance doesn't make up for Bishop Graphics' disagreeable use of copy protection, but it does eliminate system "down time" should the master disk fail.

MAKING IT WITH QUIK CIRCUIT

In order to provide a more clear picture of the operation of Quik Circuit, Figs. B-4 thru B-13 illustrate the major steps involved in the design of a PCB. This representative design is a speech synthesizer based on the SSI 263A IC.

McCAD P.C.B.

McCad P.C.B. is a PCB design environment with numerous similarities to Quik Circuit. There are differences, however, and the biggest one is McCad P.C.B.'s elaborate use of menu selections for tracings, pads, and patterns (see Fig. B-14). In short, you don't customize with McCad P.C.B., you just design. Additionally, McCad P.C.B. has the ability to output to an Apple LASERWRITER, as well as the ImageWriter and assorted plotters.

When beginning McCad P.C.B. you start at Finder, not Mini-Finder as with Quik Circuit, and double click on the McCad P.C.B. icon. Before you reach the McCad P.C.B.'s work area, you may select either a previous layout file or start a new design. These selections are made through

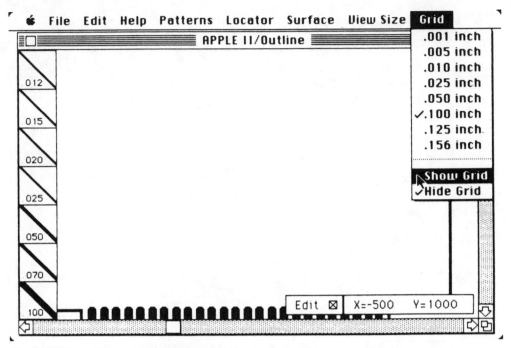

Fig. B-4. Step 1. Place a .100 inch grid over the work area.

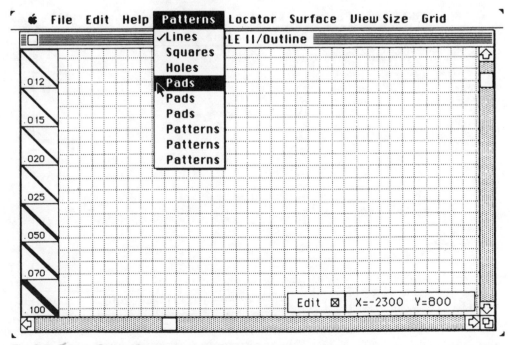

Fig. B-5. Step 2. Select IC pads from the Patterns menu.

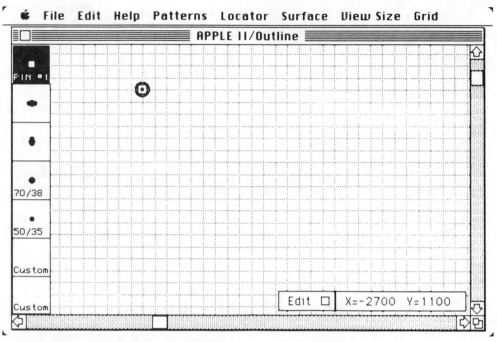

Fig. B-6. Step 3. Use the Pin #1 tool for marking the position of your IC's pin #1.

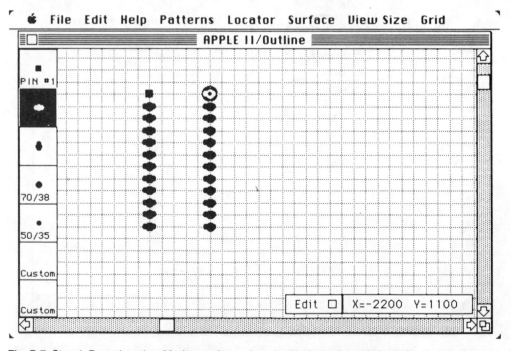

Fig. B-7. Step 4. Draw the other 23 pins on the work area with the horizontal pin pad tool.

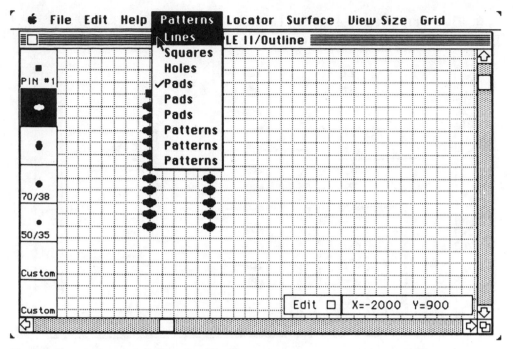

Fig. B-8. Step 5. Select trace lines from the Patterns menu.

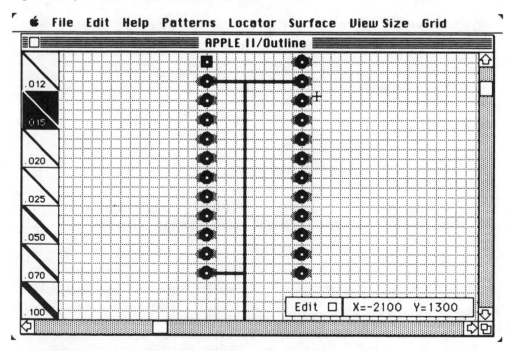

Fig. B-9. Step 6. Use the .015 tool for drawing all circuit traces.

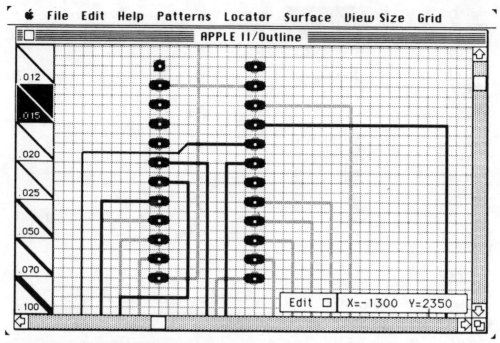

Fig. B-10. Step 7. Place overlapping traces on different sides of the PCB.

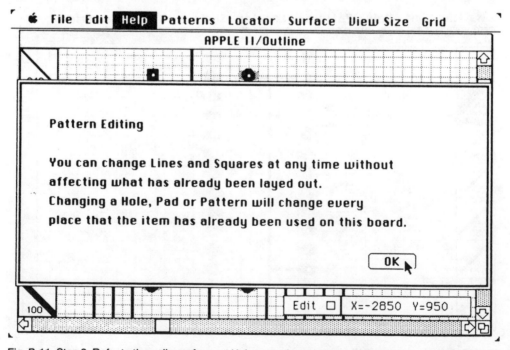

Fig. B-11. Step 8. Refer to the online reference Help menu for answers to any design questions.

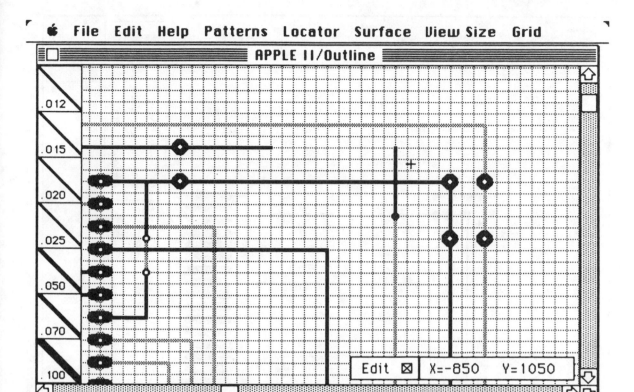

Fig. B-12. Step 9. Remove unwanted traces through selective editing.

the File menu. After you have made your selection, you are placed in the work area.

There are three tools that will make your design life that much easier. First, there is a ruler that is located along both the top and the left-hand edge of the active window. This ruler can also be printed on your final printout. You will find this to be a valuable feature during your preliminary design stages. Second, there is a variable grid that can be spread over the entire work area. The grid's size is determined through the Layout menu. This grid is essential for the exact placement of tracings, pads, and patterns. The third and last tool is a selectable magnification. There are seven different magnifications, from 20% to 1000%, that can be activated from the Scale menu. Most of these magnifications are used during an average design session. For example, when you are doing detail work, the higher magnifications are selected, whereas the lower magnifications are used in the beginning layout work.

Like its other Macintosh CAD relative, McCad P.C.B. is supplied in a utilitarian, hardbound, three-ring binder. The unique (some might

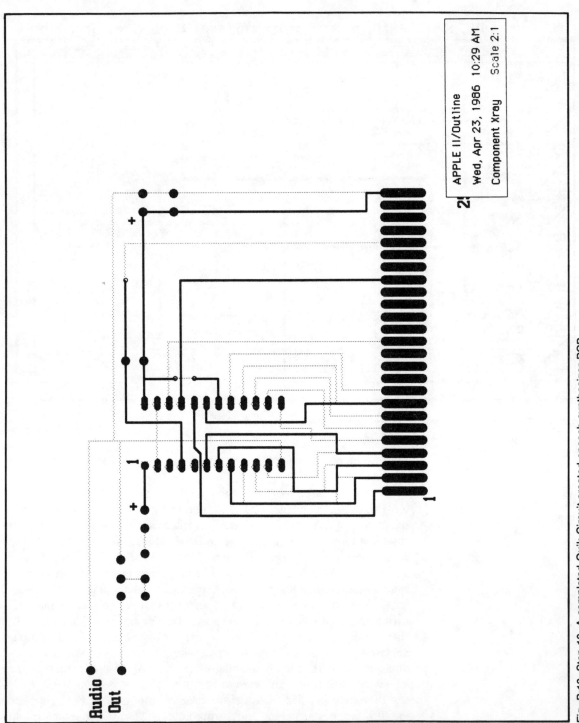

APPLE II/Outline
Wed, Apr 23, 1986 10:29 AM
Component Xray   Scale 2:1

Audio
Out

Fig. B-13. Step 10. A completed Quik Circuit-created speech synthesizer PCB.

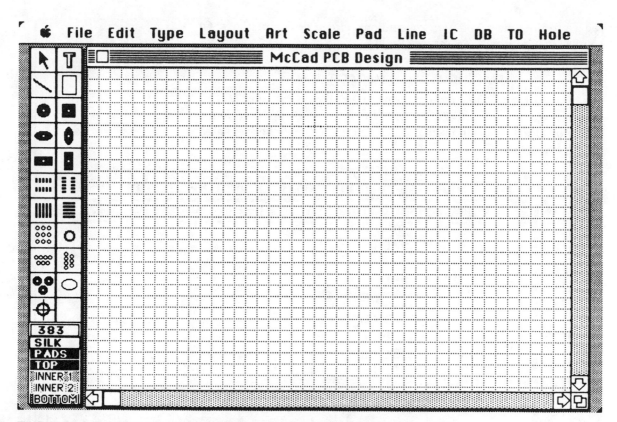

Fig. B-14. McCAD P.C.B.'s "busy" work area is vastly different from the Spartan Quik Circuit.

call odd) design of this binder excludes the need for a complementary slipcase. This comprehensive manual can be difficult to wade through in search of a solution to a design problem. Thoughtfully, VAMP has provided a short "five minute manual" for helping you quickly learn the basics of PCB design. On the issue of the software, McCad P.C.B. comes on both a master disk and a backup disk. Like Quik Circuit, these disks are copy-protected.

A major point in the favor of these two Macintosh PCB design programs is their low cost. Remarkably enough, you could purchase an entire Macintosh CAD system (i.e., 512K Mac, ImageWriter, and either Quik Circuit or McCad P.C.B.) for the same cost as AutoCAD 2. Now don't misinterpret this statement as a proclamation of equivalence between these Macintosh CAD packages and AutoCAD 2. This just isn't so. The superiority of AutoCAD 2 over both of these Macintosh programs is clearly definable. This cost factor, however, is important to many designers and is a factor in determining solutions. A better and more easily defended argument that favors all PCB design software is with regard to the time saved over conventional circuit design methods. Of course, this goes without saying. Right?

MAKING IT WITH McCAD P.C.B.

In order to provide a more clear picture of the operation of McCad P.C.B., Figs. B-15 thru B-24 illustrate the major steps involved in the design of a PCB. This representative design is a speech synthesizer based on the SSI 263A IC.

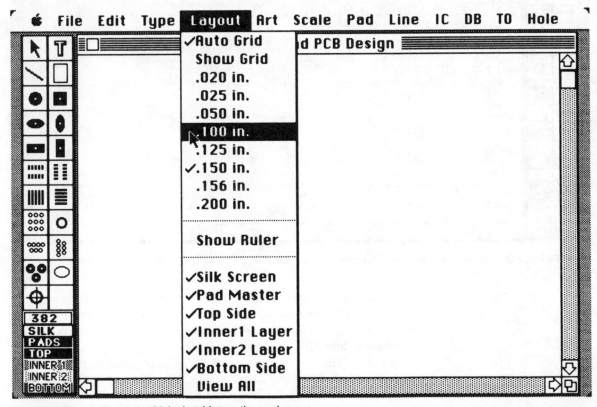

Fig. B-15. Step 1. Place a .100 inch grid over the work area.

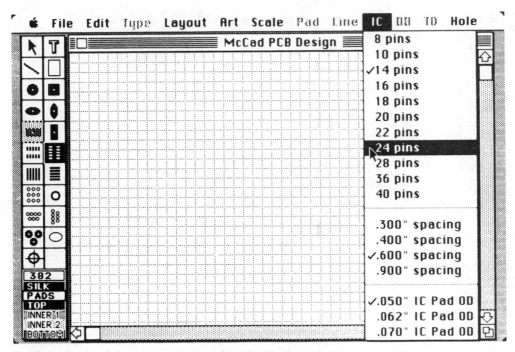

Fig. B-16. Step 2. Select a 24-pin pattern from the IC menu.

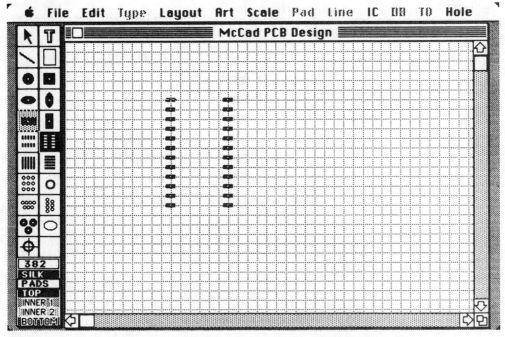

Fig. B-17. Step 3. Use the horizontal pad tool for marking the position of your IC's pin #1.

171

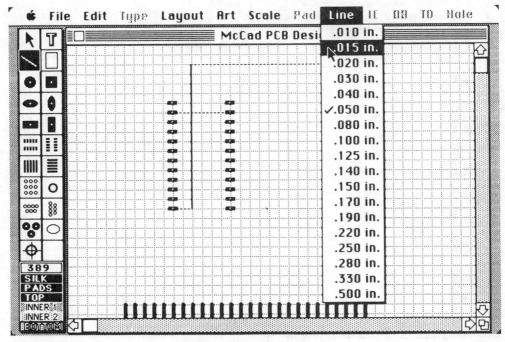

Fig. B-18. Step 4. Select .015 trace from the Line menu.

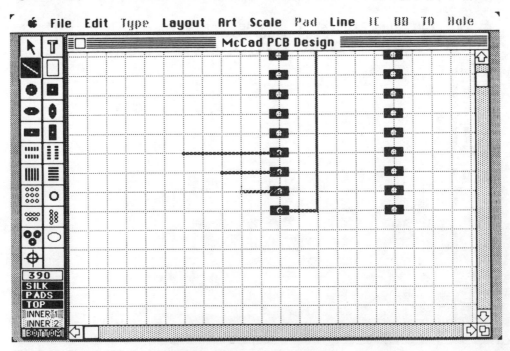

Fig. B-19. Step 5. Use the trace tool for drawing all circuit traces.

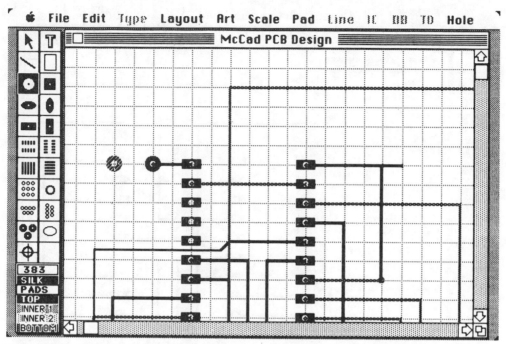

Fig. B-20. Step 6. Place overlapping traces and pads on different sides of the PCB.

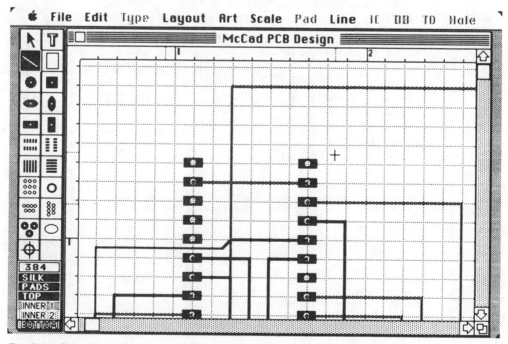

Fig. B-21. Step 7. Use the ruler option for greater precision in PCB design.

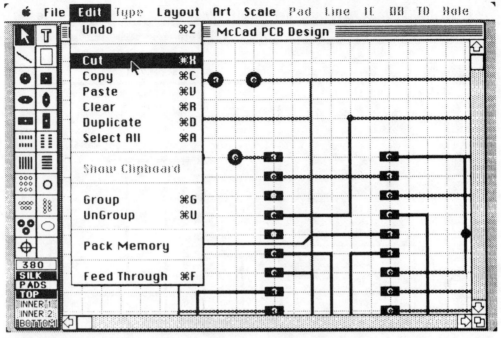

Fig. B-22. Step 8. Remove unwanted traces through selective editing.

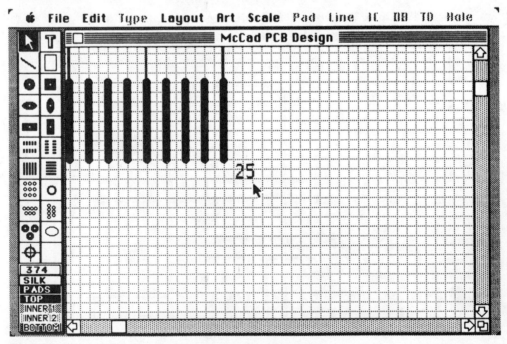

Fig. B-23. Step 9. Add lettering with the text and pointer tools.

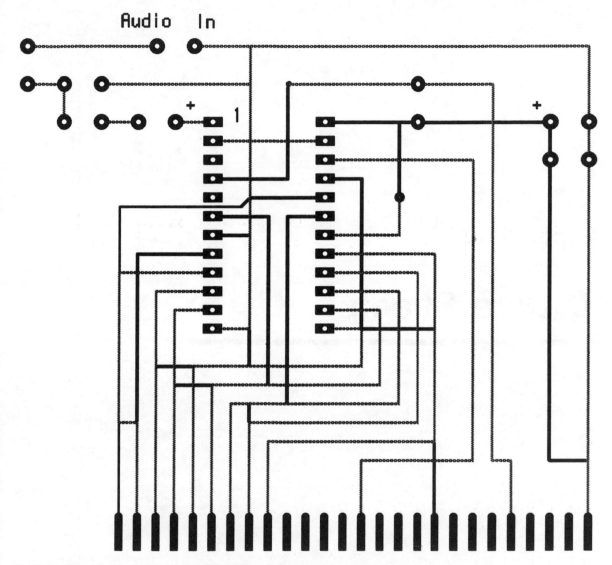

Fig. B-24. Step 10. A completed McCAD P.C.B.-created speech synthesizer PCB.

Appendix C

IC Data Sheets

4011

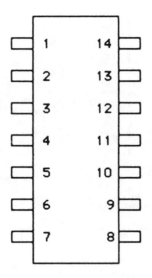

Pin Assignments			
Pin Number	Function	Pin Number	Function
1	A	8	E
2	B	9	F
3	$J = \overline{AB}$	10	$L = \overline{EF}$
4	$K = \overline{CD}$	11	$M = \overline{GH}$
5	C	12	G
6	D	13	H
7	V_{SS}	14	V_{DD}

4013

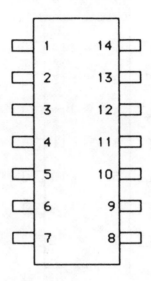

Pin Assignments			
Pin Number	Function	Pin Number	Function
1	Q1	8	Set2
2	$\overline{Q}1$	9	D2
3	Clock1	10	Reset2
4	Reset1	11	Clock2
5	D1	12	$\overline{Q}2$
6	Set1	13	Q2
7	V_{SS}	14	V_{DD}

4014

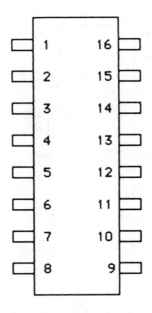

Pin Assignments			
Pin Number	Function	Pin Number	Function
1	PI-8	9	P/S CTL
2	Q6	10	Clk
3	Q8	11	Serial IN
4	PI-4	12	Q7
5	PI-3	13	PI-5
6	PI-2	14	PI-6
7	PI-1	15	PI-7
8	V_{SS}	16	V_{DD}

4024

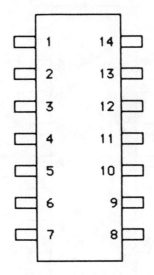

Pin Assignments			
Pin Number	Function	Pin Number	Function
1	ϕ	8	NC
2	Reset	9	$V_0 3$
3	$V_0 7$	10	NC
4	$V_0 6$	11	$V_0 2$
5	$V_0 5$	12	$V_0 1$
6	$V_0 4$	13	NC
7	V_{SS}	14	V_{DD}

4069

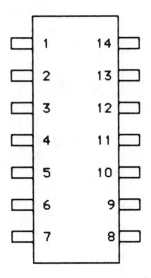

Pin Assignments			
Pin Number	Function	Pin Number	Function
1	A	8	$J = \bar{D}$
2	$G = \bar{A}$	9	D
3	B	10	$K = \bar{E}$
4	$H = \bar{B}$	11	E
5	C	12	$L = \bar{F}$
6	$I = \bar{C}$	13	F
7	V_{SS}	14	V_{DD}

4081

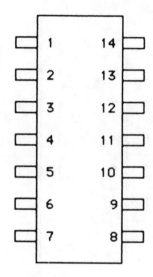

Pin Assignments			
Pin Number	Function	Pin Number	Function
1	A	8	E
2	B	9	F
3	J = A * B	10	L = E * F
4	K = C * D	11	M = G * H
5	C	12	G
6	D	13	H
7	V_{SS}	14	V_{DD}

74LS00

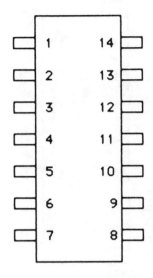

Pin Assignments			
Pin Number	Function	Pin Number	Function
1	1A	8	3Y
2	1B	9	3A
3	1Y	10	3B
4	2A	11	4Y
5	2B	12	4A
6	2Y	13	4B
7	Gnd	14	V_{CC}

7416

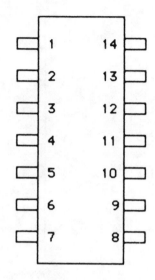

Pin Assignments			
Pin Number	Function	Pin Number	Function
1	1A	8	4Y
2	1Y	9	4A
3	2A	10	5Y
4	2Y	11	5A
5	3A	12	6Y
6	3Y	13	6A
7	Gnd	14	V_{CC}

74LS74

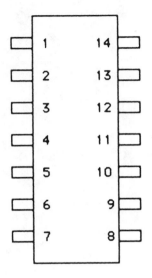

Pin Assignments			
Pin Number	Function	Pin Number	Function
1	1CLR	8	2$\overline{Q}$
2	1D	9	2Q
3	1CK	10	2PR
4	1PR	11	2CK
5	1Q	12	2D
6	1$\overline{Q}$	13	2CLR
7	Gnd	14	V_{CC}

74LS244

Pin Assignments

Pin Number	Function	Pin Number	Function
1	$\overline{1G}$	11	2A1
2	1A1	12	1Y4
3	2Y4	13	2A2
4	1A2	14	1Y3
5	2Y3	15	2A3
6	1A3	16	1Y2
7	2Y2	17	2A4
8	1A4	18	1Y1
9	2Y1	19	$\overline{2G}$
10	Gnd	20	V_{cc}

74LS373

Pin Assignments

Pin Number	Function	Pin Number	Function
1	Out Control	11	Enable G
2	1Q	12	5Q
3	1D	13	5D
4	2D	14	6D
5	2Q	15	6Q
6	3Q	16	7Q
7	3D	17	7D
8	4D	18	8D
9	4Q	19	8Q
10	Gnd	20	V_{cc}

LM386

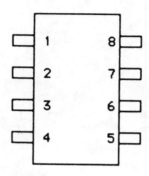

Pin Assignments	
Pin Number	Function
1	Gain
2	– Input
3	+ Input
4	Gnd
5	V_{Out}
6	V_S
7	Bypass
8	Gain

LM741

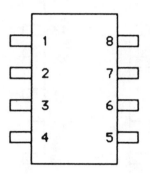

Pin Assignments	
Pin Number	Function
1	Offset Null
2	Inverting Input
3	Non-Inverting Input
4	V -
5	Offset Null
6	Output
7	V +
8	No Connection

MC1488

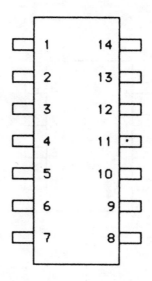

Pin Assignments			
Pin Number	Function	Pin Number	Function
1	V_{EE}	8	Output C
2	Input A	9	Input C_2
3	Output A	10	Input C_1
4	Input B_1	11	Output D
5	Input B_2	12	Input D_2
6	Output B	13	Input D_1
7	Gnd	14	V_{CC}

MC1489

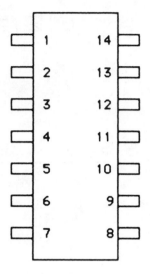

Pin Assignments			
Pin Number	Function	Pin Number	Function
1	Input A	8	Output C
2	Control A	9	Control C
3	Output A	10	Input C
4	Input B	11	Output D
5	Control B	12	Control D
6	Output B	13	Input D
7	Gnd	14	V_{CC}

MSM5204

Pin Assignments

Pin Number	Function	Pin Number	Function
1	V_R	10	Gnd
2	V_{IN}	11	D6
3	Gnd	12	D7
4	D0	13	$\overline{INT}$
5	D1	14	$\overline{RD}$
6	D2	15	$\overline{WR}$
7	D3	16	$\overline{CS}$
8	D4	17	Clk In
9	D5	18	V_{CC}

Appendix D

Supply Source Guide

REFERENCES TO A NUMBER OF UNUSUAL MATERIALS FOR CON-structing speech synthesizer projects have been made throughout this book. Because many of these materials might be difficult to find in many remote areas, this appendix provides a list of mail order houses through which these items can be purchased. Additionally, the names and addresses of specific product manufacturers are included.

Apple Computer, Incorporated
20525 Mariani Avenue
Cupertine, CA 95014
ImageWriter
LaserWriter
Apple II family of computers, including the II+, IIe, and IIc
Macintosh Computer

Autodesk, Incorporated
2658 Bridgeway
Sausalito, CA 94965
AutoCAD 2 software

Bishop Graphics, Incorporated
P. O. Box 5007
5388 Sterling Center Drive
Westlake Village, CA 91359
E-Z Circuit PC Boards (#EZ7402, #EZ7475, and #EZ7464)
E-Z Circuit Pressure-Sensitive Copper Patterns
Quik Circuit

Commodore Business Machines, Inc.
1200 Wilson Drive
West Chester, PA 19380
Amiga
Commodore 64

First Byte
2845 Temple Avenue
Long Beach, CA 90806
SmoothTalker

Heath/Zenith
Benton Harbor, MI 49022
HEROjr
Voice Synthesis Course
Texas Instruments TMS5110A Chip Set

Jameco Electronics
1355 Shoreway Road
Belmont, CA 94002
ICs
DT1050 Digitalker Chip Set

Oki Semiconductor
650 N. Mary Avenue
Sunnyvale, CA 94086
MSM5218RS
MSM5205RS
MSM6202GSK

Radio Shack Stores
General Instrument CTS256A-AL2
General Instrument SPO256-AL2
Modular Breadboard Socket

RC Systems, Inc.
121 West Winesap Road
Bothell, WA 98012
Slot-Buster

Scott Electronics Supply Corporation
4895 F Street
Omaha, NE 68117
Ungar System 9000
Weller EC2000 Soldering Station

Sig Manufacturing Company, Incorporated
401 South Front Street
Montezuma, IA 50171
Aeroplastic ABS plastic sheeting
Clear Plastic Sheets
X-Acto Saw Blades (#234)

Sweet Micro Systems
50 Freeway Drive
Cranston, RI 02920
Mockingboard B

Tower Hobbies
P. O. Box 778
Champaign, IL 61820
Satellite City's Super "T" cyanoacrylate adhesive

VAMP, Inc.
6753 Selma Avenue
Los Angeles, CA 90028
McCAD P.C.B.

Vector Electronics Company, Inc.
12460 Gladstone Avenue
Sylmar, CA 91342
Vector Plugboards

Votrax, Inc.
1394 Rankin
Troy, MI 48083-4074
Votrax Personal Speech System
Votrax SC-01

Wahl Clipper Corporation
2902 Locust Street
Sterling, IL 61081
Isotip Soldering Irons (#7800, #7700, and #7240)

Bibliography

BOOKS

Abernathy, E., 1970, *Fundamentals of Speech Communication*, Wm. C. Brown Company Publishers, Dubuque, IA
-an elementary introduction to the basics of speech and, primarily, communication

Elovitz, H. S., R. W. Johnson, A. McHugh, and J. E. Shore, 1976, *Automatic Translation of English Text to Phonetics by Means of Letter to Sound Rules*, United States Naval Research Laboratory Report 7948
-this is the original study that is the basis for most of today's text-to-speech algorithms

Engelsher, C. J., 1984, *Interfacing & Digital Experiments with Your Apple*, TAB Books, Blue Ridge Summit, PA
-all of the elemental electronics that you will need to know for plugging a speech synthesizer into your Apple computer

Freud, S., (1916-1917) 1974, *Introductory Lectures on Psychoanalysis*, Translated by J. Strachey, Penguin Books, Harmondsworth, England
-an English reprint of the classic Sigmund Freud work

Fromkin, V.A. (editor), 1980, *Errors in Linguistic Performance, Slips of the Tongue, Ear, Pen, and Hand*, Academic Press, New York, NY
-a series of papers that explore the reasons behind verbal screw ups

Jones, D., 1950, *The Phoneme: Its Nature and Use*, W. Heffer & Sons, Cambridge, England
-the classic text of phonetic definitions

Kramer, C.E. and R. West, 1960, *Phonetics*, Harper & Brothers, New York, NY
-an introductory speech book that provides vocal mechanism illustrations showing the production of many different phonemes

Kuecken, J. A., 1983, *Talking Computers and Telecommunications*, Van Nostrand Reinhold, New York, NY
-speech synthesis from a telecommunications point of view

Leibson, S., 1983, *The Handbook of Microcomputer Interfacing*, TAB Books, Blue Ridge Summit, PA
-an excellent introduction to the electronics of parallel and serial connections

Lieberman, P., 1972, *The Speech of Primates*, Mouton & Co. N. V. Publishers, The Hague, Netherlands
-a collection of papers covering the biology and physiology of human and non-human speech

Lieberman, P., 1977, *Speech Physiology and Acoustic Phonetics*, MacMillan Publishing Co., Inc., New York, NY
-an emphasis on the relationships between the biology of the vocal mechanism and the electronics of speech synthesis

Rabiner, L.R. and R.W. Schafer, 1978, *Digital Processing of Speech Signals*, Prentice-Hall, Inc., Englewood Cliffs, NJ
-a technical look at the formulas of the different speech synthesis techniques

Rigsby, M., 1982, *Verbal Control with Microcomputers*, TAB Books, Blue Ridge Summit, PA
-complete hardware and software instructions for the construction of a TRS-80 Model I speech recognition system

Steele, R., 1975, *Delta Modulation Systems*, Halsted Press, London, England
-all of the equations that you will ever want to see for DM systems

Tedeschi, F. P. and R. Colon, 1983, *101 Projects for the Z80*, TAB Books, Blue Ridge Summit, PA
-hardware and software projects geared for the SD-Z80 System

Teja, E.R. and G.W. Gonnella, 1983, *Voice Technology*, Reston Publishing Co., Inc., Reston, VA
-an introductory examination of speech synthesis with very little practical application

MAGAZINE ARTICLES

Anderson, 1981, "An Extremely Low-Cost Computer Voice Response System," BYTE, FEB 1981, p. 36

Ciarcia, 1978, "Talk to Me! Add a Voice to Your Computer for $35," BYTE, JUN 1978, p. 142

Ciarcia, 1981, "Build a Low-Cost Speech Synthesizer Interface," BYTE, JUN 1981, p. 46

Ciarcia, 1981, "Build an Unlimited-Vocabulary Speech Synthesizer," BYTE SEP 1981, p. 38

Ciarcia, 1982, "Use Voiceprints to Analyse Speech," BYTE, MAR 1982, p.50

Ciarcia, 1982, "Build the Microvox Text-to-Speech Synthesizer, Part I," BYTE, SEP 1982, p. 64; ". . . Part 2," BYTE, OCT 1982, p. 40

Ciarcia, 1983, "Use ADPCM for Highly Intelligible Speech Synthesis," BYTE, JUN 1983, p. 35

Ciarcia, 1984, "Build a Third-Generation Phonetic Speech Synthesizer," BYTE, MAR 1984, p. 28

Ciarcia, 1984, "The Lis'ner 1000," BYTE, NOV 1984, p. 110

Hoot, 1983, "Voice Lab, Part 1: A System for Digital Speech Synthesis and Analysis," BYTE, JUL 1983, p. 186

Hoot, 1983, "Voice Lab, Part 2: Menu-Driven Routines for Digital Speech Synthesis and Analysis," BYTE, AUG 1983, p. 456

O'Haver, 1978, "Audio Processing with a Microcomputer," BYTE, JUN 1978, p. 166

Smith, 1984, "Five Voice Synthesizers," BYTE, SEP 1984, p. 337

Glossary

address—the location in memory where a given binary bit or word of information is stored.

affricate consonant—the sound of a fricative that follows a plosive.

allophone—two or more variants of the same phoneme.

alphanumeric—the set of alphabetic, numeric, and punctuation characters used for computer input.

analog/digital (A/D) conversion—a device that measures incoming voltages and outputs a corresponding digital number for each voltage.

ASCII—American Standard Code for Information Interchange.

assembly language—a low level symbolic programming language that comes close to programming a computer in its internal machine language.

binary—the base two number system, in which 1 and 0 represent the on and off states of a circuit.

bit—one binary digit.

byte—a group of eight bits.

chip—an integrated circuit.

consonant—a phoneme that is formed through a constricted vocal passage.

continuant—a fixed position that is held during phonation.

CPU—Central Processing Unit; the major operations center of the computer where decisions and calculations are made.

CMOS—a complementary metal oxide semiconductor IC that contains both P-channel and N-channel MOS transistors.

data—information that the computer operates on.

data rate—the amount of data transmitted through a communications line per unit of time.

debug—to remove program errors, or bugs, from a program.

digital—a circuit that has only two states, on and off, which are usually represented by the binary number system.

diphthong—a gliding phoneme moving from one vowel position to another.

disk—the magnetic media on which computer programs and data are stored.

DOS—Disk Operating System; allows the use of general commands to manipulate the data stored on a disk.

EPROM—an erasable programmable read-only memory semiconductor that can be user-programmed.

firmware—software instructions permanently stored within a computer using a read only memory (ROM) device.

floppy disk—see disk.

flowchart—a diagram of the various steps to be taken by a computer in running a program.

fricative—a consonant forced through a narrow, frictional vocal passage.

glide—the uninterrupted movement from one speech sound position to another.

hardware—the computer and its associated peripherals, as opposed to the software programs that the computer runs.

hexadecimal—a base sixteen number system often used in programming in assembly language.

input—to send data into a computer.

input/output (I/O) devices—peripheral hardware devices that exchange information with a computer.

interface—a device that converts electronic signals to enable communications between two devices; also called a port.

languages—the set of words and commands that are understood by the computer and used in writing a program.

loop—a programming technique that allows a portion of a program to be repeated several times.

LSI—a layered semiconductor fabricated from approximately 10,000 discrete devices.

machine language—the internal, low level language of the computer.

memory—an area within a computer reserved for storing data and programs that the computer can operate on.

microcomputer—a small computer, such as the Commodore Amiga, that contains all of the instructions it needs to operate on a few internal integrated circuits.

mnemonic—an abbreviation or word that represents another word or phrase.

MOS—a metal oxide semiconductor containing field-effect MOS transistors.

nasal—a speech sound produced through the nasal cavity.

NMOS—an N-channel metal oxide semiconductor with N-type source and drain diffusions in a P substrate.

octal—a base eight number system often used in machine language programming.

opcode—an operation code signifying a particular task to be performed by the computer.

parallel port—a data communications channel that sends data out along several wires, so that entire bytes can be transmitted simultaneously, rather than by one single bit at a time.

peripheral—an external device that communicates with a computer, such as a printer, a modem, or a disk drive.

phoneme—the basic speech sound.

PMOS—a P-channel metal oxide semiconductor with P-type source and drain diffusions in an N substrate.

program—a set of instructions for the computer to perform.

RAM—Random Access Memory; integrated circuits within the computer where data and programs can be stored and recalled. Data stored within RAM is lost when the computer's power is turned off.

ROM—Read-Only Memory; integrated circuits which permanently store data or programs. The information contained on a ROM chip cannot be changed and is not lost when the computer's power is turned off.

RS-232C—a standard form for serial computer interfaces.

serial communications—a method of data communication in which bits of information are sent consecutively through one wire.

software—a set of programmed instructions that the computer must execute.

statement—a single computer instruction.

subroutine—a small program routine contained within a larger program.

terminal—an input/output device that uses a keyboard and a video display.

vowel—a phoneme that is produced from an open, unrestricted vocal mechanism.

word—a basic unit of computer memory usually expressed in terms of a byte.

Index

Index

Other Best Sellers From TAB

☐ **C PROGRAMMING—WITH BUSINESS APPLICATIONS—Dr. Leon A. Wortman and Thomas O. Sidebottom**

This learn-by-doing guide puts its emphasis on actual programs that demonstrate the ways C code is entered, manipulated, and modified to achieve specific applications goals. Also included are sample runs for many of the programs and a disk containing all of the book's programs, for use on the IBM PC/XT/AT and compatibles with at least 256K. 260 pp., 95 illus.

Paper **$18.95**　　　　　　　　　　　Hard **$25.95**
Book No. 2857

☐ **TURBO PASCAL® TOOLBOX—A Programmer's Guide—Paul Garrison**

In this FIRST and ONLY, in-depth look at the Turbo modules, veteran computer author Paul Garrison gives you the data you need to decide which of the Turbo Pascal toolbox modules offer the programming features you need, and how to make full use of the modules once you make your purchase. Writing in clear, easy-to-follow style, he includes over **200 example programs, procedures, and subroutines** on topics ranging from word processing and database handling to color graphics and games. 288 pp., 207 illus.

Paper **$17.95**　　　　　　　　　　　Hard **$25.95**
Book No. 2852

☐ **WORKING WITH SUPERCALC® 4—Jerry Willis and William Pasewark**

Up-to-date instructions for using new SuperCalc 4 to organize and manage data for business and financial applications. Now IBM® PC and compatible users can quickly organize, arrange, and manipulate all types of information using the new and vastly improved SuperCalc 4, one of the top software packages on the market today! This comprehensive guide shows you how to use this powerful electronic spreadsheet for all your own personal applications needs. Packed with applications data and actual example programs! 300 pp., 125 illus.

Paper **$18.95**　　　　　　　　　　　Hard **$24.95**
Book No. 2814

☐ **FRAMEWORK II™ APPLICATIONS—2nd Edition —Richard H. Baker**

This invaluable, revised edition shows you how to get the most out of Framework II's vastly improved communications facilities, its strengthened word processor, and its larger spreadsheet. And you'll learn how to do most of it by direct command using one of Framework's unique functions called "Idea Processing." This feature allows you to think about information as you do naturally, instead of trying to conform to the needs of your computer. 336 pp., 218 illus.

Paper **$19.95**　　　　　　　　　　　Hard **$26.95**
Book No. 2798

☐ **C PROGRAMMER'S UTILITY LIBRARY —Frank Whitsell**

Here's a sourcebook that goes beyond simple programming techniques to focus on the efficient use of system resources to aid in the development of higher quality C programs! It's a unique collection of ready-to-use functions and utilities! There's also a ready-to-run disk available for use on the IBM PC/XT/AT and compatibles with at least 256K. 200 pp., 268 illus.

Paper **$16.95**　　　　　　　　　　　Hard **$24.95**
Book No. 2855

☐ **MICROCOMPUTER APPLICATIONS DEVELOPMENT: TECHNIQUES FOR EVALUATION AND IMPLEMENTATION—Michael Simon Bodner, and Pamela Kay Hutchins**

This comprehensive guide represents an overview of the process of application development in the microcomputer environment from BOTH a technical methodology and a business issues point of view. The authors introduce the steps involved in applications development: as well as numerous shortcuts and development tips that they have learned over the years. You'll get invaluable insight into the various types of projects you may encounter. 256 pp., 69 illus.

Hard **$24.95**　　　　　　　　　　　Book No. 2840

☐ **dBASE III® PLUS: ADVANCED APPLICATIONS FOR NONPROGRAMMERS—Richard H. Baker**

The new dBASE III PLUS makes all the advantages offered by dBASE as a programming language incredibly easy even for the non-programmer. And to make it even simpler for you to program like a pro, dBASE expert Richard Baker leads you painlessly through each programming step. Focusing on the practical rather than the theoretical aspects of programming, he explores dBASE III PLUS on three levels—entry level, intermediate, and experienced. 448 pp., 232 illus.

Paper **$19.95**　　　　　　　　　　　Hard **$27.95**
Book No. 2808

☐ **MAXIMUM PERFORMANCE WITH LOTUS® 1-2-3®, Versions 1.0 and 2.0—Robin Stark and Stuart Leitner**

Going far beyond the material covered in ordinary user's manuals, the authors provide expert techniques, shortcuts, and programming tips gleaned from their own experience and the experience of others who have reached "power-user" status in 1-2-3 operation. Included are "10 tricks every Lotus user should know" and "10 common worksheet problems and how to solve them!" 250 pp., 96 illus.

Paper **$17.95**　　　　　　　　　　　Hard **$25.95**
Book No. 2771

Other Best Sellers From TAB